Cadence Collective: Year One Anthology

Cadence Collective: Year One Anthology

Best of CadenceCollective.net
from August 2013 to July 2014
Poets from, near, and influenced by
Long Beach, California

Table of Contents

Quarter 1:   August, September, October

Quarter 2: November, December, January

Quarter 3: February, March, April

Quarter 4: May, June, July

More information and individual biographies for poets can be found at cadencecollective.net/poets/

Cadence Collective Team

Editor-in-Chief
Sarah Thursday

Assistant Anthology Editors
Terry Wright and Nancy Lynée Woo

Anthology Selection Committee
Terry Wright, Jax NTP, Fernando Gallegos, Denise R. Weuve, John Brantingham, Christian Lozada, Mickie Lynn, Danielle Mitchell, Robbi Nester, G. Murray Thomas, Nancy Lynée Woo, Alisha Attella, Alejandro Duarte, LeAnne Hunt, Jackie Joice, Frank Kearns, Elmast Kozloyan, Karie McNeley, Raquel Reyes-Lopez, and Thomas R. Thomas

Anthology Cover Art
"Flowers" by Esmeralda Villalobos

Yearbook Portrait Series
Fernando Gallegos

Website Editorial Team
Denise R. Weuve and Raquel Reyes-Lopez

Monthly Website Art
Esmeralda Villalobos

Gratitude

Thank you to the amazing poetry and artistic community in Long Beach, including Alyssandra Nighswonger and Viento Y Agua Coffeehouse, Danielle Mitchell and The Poetry Lab, G. Murray Thomas, Sean Moor of Gatsby Books, all the hosts and participants of open mics across town, website and anthology volunteers, Esmeralda Villalobos, Fernando Gallegos, generous contributors, and faithful readers.

Introduction

It would be foolish to make the claim that Long Beach writing is homogeneous in its approach to style or subject matter, but something in it certainly distinguishes it as its own literary movement. There are a number of reasons for its style. Not the least of which are its early figures, Charles Bukowski, Gerald Locklin, Joan Jobe Smith, Marilyn Johnson, Fred Voss, and several others. They were like-minded people whose styles grew out of a mutual appreciation. They developed together and out of literary magazines such as *Pearl, Chiron Review,* and *Nerve Cowboy,* and collections like Charles Harper Webb's *Stand Up Poetry,* which helps to define who these poets were and are in relation to a larger national movement.

So how can one define Long Beach area poetry? There are some key elements that its practitioners tend to follow or meaningfully resist. Long Beach poets tend to prefer the short word to the long. Most of what they are doing is at least on one level immediately relatable. Even when people are half-drunk and hearing it out loud in a crowded bar, they will be moved to laugh, sneer, or cry because of it. At its best, however, there are several layers of meaning that makes each reading a powerful experience. Those who read Donna Hilbert's or Daniel McGinn's poetry again and again begin to realize that poems about the beach or traffic or a sad little man in a bar can be expanded into tracts about the meaning of existence.

Readings, bars, and venues have vied for the central position as Long Beach's poetry centers. A little more than a year ago, Sarah Thursday helped to define and shape the Long Beach poetry movement by creating the *Cadence Collective* website. It has been able to pull these various locations together, giving the community definition by showcasing poets from, near, and influenced by the Long Beach poetry scene.

It began with a conversation Sarah had with Danielle Mitchell at her salon, The Poetry Lab. Danielle gave Sarah the idea to create a central website that does two things at once. *Cadence Collective* is both a community hub and an online magazine. Any event in Long Beach related to poetry is catalogued here, and so it has become the first stop poets make when searching for something to do. As a magazine, Sarah has made the bold choice to showcase one poem each day that is previously published or not, from Long Beach area writers, allowing them to send her their best work. She especially enjoys publishing new and emerging talent. The result is a satisfying read every single time.

This anthology highlights the best of the website's first full year. It will move you in surprising ways. It should be read more than once. Under the seeming simplicity of these poems are meanings to be unlocked and understood. Read one in the morning, and it will stay with you all day until you find yourself opening it again before you go to bed.

That's the common-sense genius of *Cadence Collective*. It is one of the best magazines I've read in many years for one simple rule: Sarah Thursday wants only the best work poets have to offer. This anthology is the result of that insight and her great work.

John Brantingham

Quarter 1:
August, September, October

"Your Kidney Just Arrived At LAX"

G. Murray Thomas

The doctor told me as I lay in pre-op prep.
I envisioned a special chartered flight,
an entire airplane filled with organs.

Hearts with little heart shaped carry-ons.
They always watch the inflight movie
and cry all the way through.

Livers splurging on one last drink;
they don't think they'll be allowed
where they're going.

The lungs eye the spot
where the oxygen masks drop.

Corneas stare out at the passing countryside;
they always get a window seat.

The spleens are always complaining
      about security
      about the length of the flight
      about the lack of leg room
      (although they have no legs).

The gall bladder always gets in line
before his row is called.

And there's my kidney,
no doubt reading a book to pass the time
something classic: As I Lay Dying,
      or Great Expectations,
      or The Stranger.

All of them wondering
about the journey ahead,
about their new home,
about their new life.

Dancing In The Laundromat

Denise R. Weuve

We noticed the swish
of the washing machines
we sat on. Fingers,
mine, began tapping
on the metal slot
that ate our quarters.
I heard your foot
clicking against
the mustard colored machines
and looked up.
Black hair
clung to your shiny
olive forehead. Yes
it was hot; I could
feel the stickiness
of sweat on my neck.
Eyebrows arching, you smiled,
hopped down to the white
tile floor, littered
with empty Downy
bottles, and Clorox
bleach containers.
You took my wrist pulled
me to you, wrapped your
arms around my back
and began to rocking.
I blushed watching
the eyes of middle
aged woman grow
with each clumsy step
you led me into.
You kicked away a soap
box to free our path
as we twirled and spun.

The only eyes I saw
then were yours, a swirl
of green that lifted
me until we were
spinning and spinning
and the dryers had
stopped to stare.

Find a Way

Faith Gobeli

"I'm frustrated," you said,
Trying to read me,
Toiling to unfold a map
That was too big to tell anything,
That was only a cacophony of directions,
Of arrows clanging like swords.

"It's okay," I answered.
"It's just how it is."
My voice fell into a tiny hole in the telephone
And crawled into your ear,
And into your tenderness.

"What we have," you replied,
"I don't want to lose what we have."
You set the words before me like a road,
Like wildflowers,
Like open air,
Like the first step in a tentative sunrise.

But I'm not good at this.

"It's life," I said.
"Things change, we have to accept it."
It's a comment that clunks like a stone.
It's a blindfold tied too tight,
A bewildering twirl
At the bottom of towering treetops.
It's forgetting to ask why.

So you implore me:
"See what you're doing right now?
You're pushing me away."
There is a pause, the tapping of my foot.

Then there is you,
And your feet moving,
Climbing to the top of my silence,
To where you can wave arms,
To where you can shout
and draw an X in the sand.

But I don't tell you
That I don't know how.
I don't tell you
That not knowing hurts.

Instead, I let you drift with me
And hope the current will be kind
Enough
To carry us in the same direction.

Dinner at Lola's

Alisha Attella

There was a moment that I missed in between
days when my kids became something else.
They chatter and whinny and laugh now
telling stories of their life beyond me.

Elbows to the table, I sit and listen and ask the good questions
I watch the tipped old man smile in our direction
I raise cheers with my $4 beer and their fancy kid cups
And make slow eyes at the waiter with the mule-heart tattoo

There was one night that I remember so clear,
I ordered the first pizza that came to our place.
The boy brought it in one of those hot bags.
His little stitched visor looked just like a crown.

The kids were smaller then and they pooled to our door,
so proud presenting the money to King Domino.
Dollars to ransom our time from the kitchen,
and from the days, so close behind, where there was
too much work and Mom was wet sand
heavy because things weren't ever enough.

So now, it's dinner at Lola's on the short drive home,
and these little people sitting with me don't remember
the first ransomed night, criss-cross-applesauce
on the floor with a big cheap pizza, because now
pennies are saved aside for these nights, pinched
so that once a week I can buy moments outright

Six bucks for my dreamy daughter framed by trumpet red blooms,
another six for my son with a forkful of confetti-bright rice,
and just a few pennies more to see them hang, suspended
in mid-bite forever, while they talk about the lines in the sky.

A Poem is Not a Teddy Bear

Clint Margrave

after Tony Hoagland and for him

Nor is it polite, or pretty, or politically correct.
A poem is not a liberal or a Democrat.
A poem is not a Republican either, or a Libertarian.
A poem is not from a particular region of France
or from the East or West.
A poem is not black or white or Scandinavian.
A poem gets angry, feels contempt, lies sometimes.
You can't hold it close to your chest
or snuggle up to it.
A poem is not running for president.
It doesn't need your vote or want to be your friend.
A poem is a ferocious animal, drool dripping
down its chin—
not a blanky to take to grandma's house
or a tissue to wipe your nose with.
A poem is not a teddy bear,
but if it were would come unstitched,
dragged too often in the dirt,
too many nights forgotten in the wet cold,
abandoned, decapitated, dumped off,
or chewed up in games of tug of war.
The kind you keep banished to your closet
once you've grown,
cover up its foul old stench
with elegant perfumes and colognes.
The kind that in the minds of others does not exist,
that's been kept hidden so long
scares the shit out of you
when the light from outside shines in,
and you forget what it is.

My Heaven

Donna Hilbert
for Lenore Brown

In my heaven I wear
white cashmere Armani,
eat chocolate truffles
without dribbling my breasts.
The more Camels I smoke
the better my breath smells
and Cosmos and cabernet—
all the fruit that I wish.
Every day here is Great Hair Day
and I always look ravishing,
rested and thin. There are no duties
in heaven, just one long salon
with talk unfailingly brilliant.
Infinitely witty and quick
come to mind. No sputtering
world for tiresome distraction. Up here,
down there doesn't come up for discussion.
Life in heaven: endless insouciance,
all bon mots and bonbons.
Did I mention how superb is my French?
And what of my poems?
Now, Major Movies.
Every one sold for Big Bucks
and starring in all The Roles of a Lifetime
is my favorite actress,
the incomparable, inimitable,
lovable Me.

August 14th

Karie McNeley

When you forget your lover's
birthday, don't try to make up
for it. No sweet excuses.
No happy belateds! Just
no! If it's only been a
day or two, let it slither
into three, then four, then ten,
thirty, eighty. She'll never
notice. Soon enough the year
will have passed like laundry and
countless dishes, and you'll be
back at that horrible day.
Your love will be a whole year
older, fatter, wiser, and
a lot dumber too. And though
your memory has not really
improved. You've grown more aware.
And this time, you'll notice the
cool icing on her stone lips,
the T-shirt she is wearing
that isn't yours, the lustful
bruise on her neck. You'll ask her
what sharp secret she's holding
behind her back. And a grin,
wicked and still, will distort
her face as you say "Happy—

Kings River Blues (Part One)

Jackie Joice

This poem isn't about sunsets and sunrise
or landscapes and otherwise.
It's about the blood of grapes and hard
labor, sweat, and bone in scorching fields,
accompanied by cheap wages for picking
pounds and pounds of cotton and grapes.
Wine grapes that were processed with
mechanical feet,
smashed.
It's about blood-speckled white afro puffs
being picked for Rodeo Drive clothing
stores.
It's about white afro puffs being picked to
the hymns of harmonicas bought in Texas
for twenty-five cents.
It's about whore rates for seamstresses
working twelve hours straight,
blood from Dust Bowl survivors.
Migrating
herd
hooves
sheep
like cattle packed in tents with grit.
It's solely about the perspective of a
dislocated
city chick to country parents,
but not country like down in the Mississippi
Delta country,
but Central California country.
This poem is no click of your boots to the
Midwest type of Oz.
This poem is about the heartland of
California,
about bodies in fields, picking green grapes
with black hands.

I siphon whiskey from these grapes,
and now I am drunk with
the Kings River Blues.

whore

Denise R. Weuve

she is doing it again
leaving behind
the needles,
her discarded lovers,
one after another,
a trail to her other
side, the side
that is not a mother.
the side that never
wanted to be a
mother.
her breast have
always been dry
empty sex toys
she displays
on merchant marine
ships like green cards
for the asian sailors.
she will sit in bars
for hours sending
watered down drinks
to men eating balutt.
the duckling ready
to hatch but boiled
just before the bill
could form.
It makes her ill
watching them peel
away the flesh
place the still closed
eyes on their tongues.
she forgives them all,
those mouths being
the ones she will kiss
for fifty dollars,
300 if she stays
the night.

her daughter will
figure this out soon
drop the needles
from the air
like chinese fortune
sticks that explain her fate.
then spend the night
with a georgian boy
ask for twenty dollars
knowing this is what
all women do
in smaller amounts.

Projects Prayer

J.D. Isip

She never seemed to sleep:
Mornings she wore the green oil factory shirt,
Nights the blue smock with Sav-On on a patch,
all day a troubled look, like the hunted
who pause for a breath and prop up their ears
and plot in seconds their next ten moves...

"Say your prayers" and we listened
Though we prayed for our father and he never came
and we prayed for more food and a home
and God seemed always too busy to hear
but we prayed, because, well, that's what you do
to ward off the Hate..

The Hate is what made Danny Boy start taking crystal
and his sister started sleeping around, to make a few bucks
and It is the only meal you are sure to get here
in the Projects, and maybe the missionary food
that comes every few months, when the last batch of poor people
wise up and stop praying... and they need more offerings.

"Say your prayers" and I did:
I said, "God, you bastard,
Bless my brother, that he might stop drinking for one night,
Bless my father that he might come back to us,
Bless my sister that she will not be ashamed of us,
Bless my mother that she might not wake up to your lie,
Bless You when you answer to *me*."

She never seemed to sleep:
Mornings she watched me eat the Hate
Nights she watched the Hate eat me
all day, a troubled look...

Crows

Steven Hendrix

Crows work with such precision,
the quarter-sized hole in the rabbit's side
the only evidence that they'd been there.
I pick up the rabbit which is nothing now
but skin and bones, its insides
having been removed and eaten.
I work with less precision than the crows,
dropping the rabbit before getting it
in the plastic bag, then missing the trashcan
with my first toss and finally just dropping it in.

Mustard and Ketchup

Mickie Lynn

Little one
With mustard stains
And splotches of ketchup
Across your cheek

A smile creeps in
At the corner of your mouth
What wondrous daydreams
Dance through your head?

Dragons prancing with the fairies
In a magical wonderland
A reenactment of a favored cartoon,
Each character playing his part
Crazy colored creatures wildly
Racing in metallic covered boats
Pirate sword fights, talking frogs,
And tinkling silly songs

As I ponder the possibilities...

A small finger touches the plate
Then a flurry of swirling designs
Create an exuberant energy and
The representation of ketchup
In a painting on your plate

Pigments of red and yellow
Merge to match the nectarine
Beside your napkin
A Picasso portrayal of condiments

And the smile becomes a wholehearted laugh

The Morning After

G. Murray Thomas

The room reeked of stale poetry.
There was poetry spilled all over the carpet.
The kitchen counter was covered with aluminum cans
    half full of warm poetry
    with cigarette butts floating in it.
And my head ached
    with that particular sharp pain
    that only comes from worn out neurons
    abused with too much imagined brilliance
    inspired by an excessive consumption
    of poetry.
So I sat down and
    - what else -
    cracked open a cold poem.

Poem to the Child Who Was Almost My Son

John Brantingham

Today I will tell you the stories that I have kept to myself on purpose. I will tell you of the day I hiked the mountain by myself, and I veered off the path and climbed straight up to the crest. There was a clearing in the trees and wild rose bushes growing up in the sun. The afternoon warmth and smell of pine drowsed me, so I lay down and drifted off, only to wake up to nap amnesia and a world of roses before me. And I will tell you about the time I opened the scar on my leg, climbing a fence in the September Santa Ana heat. I sat down in the weeds of a vacant lot and watched the line of red form and drip and pool, and I smiled to see it, but I don't know why, and I didn't know then. I will tell you all the stories that I never meant to tell anyone, the stories that were so precious I kept them hidden. I will tell them to you now because your other father, the man you will always know as father, the man who will give you everything else, cannot give these to you, and I will give them to no one else but you. So I will give you the day when I wandered outside alone at night for the first time in my young life, and I bent my neck back, and I became an astronomer, and I will give you the moment I crushed the bones in my arm in frustration and horror, and I will give you the moment I felt you move inside your mother, and I was sure you would be my son forever.

My Father's Brain

Clint Margrave

I'm looking at my father's brain.

My sister and I found it
stuffed in an envelope
in my parents' garage
yesterday.

Only weeks before,
it had been alive,
now it was here,
stacked in this box,
with all the other
stuff we don't know
what to do with.

"That's the frontal lobe," my sister says,
picking it up
and turning it around
to show me.

"Can I keep it?" I say,
lifting it into the sun
for a better glimpse.

"Do whatever you want with it,"
she tells me.
"It's yours."

Old Man at the Pool

Donna Hilbert

What I knew about beauty,
the summer I turned ten,
I learned from books—
how Mammy squeezed Scarlett
into her corset for that famous
hand-span waist.
I was shaped like a milk carton.
I wore my mother's old merry widow
under my bathing suit
to push me up and cinch me in.

In the pool I played water babies,
pretending I was a creature
with no earthly life.
I sat on the bottom of the pool
until the need for air
propelled me to the surface
where I would turn over and over,
somersault into exhaustion.

I don't remember his face, just the gray
wires that grew down his belly
disappearing into his black trunks.
This old man, who held me
like a bowling ball,
his thumb in my crotch,
fingers splayed across
the bald arc of my pelvis,
this man who tossed me
into deep, deep water.

Hank Williams Drives His Truck into a Tree

Larry Duncan

Hank Williams drives his truck into a tree.
The front fender carves a frayed
smile into the bark of the oak.
He can't decide if it's an omen
or the universe breeching
the veil to laugh in his face.
Either way, he has miles to go.

The engine's running
but the front axil's broke.
He can't control
the way the wheels turn.
There's no choice
but to continue the rest of the way
on foot, to leave the radio on
until the battery dies
and everything goes dark.

He knows the way to go,
down the epileptic rows of corn
turned blue by the moon
to the crossroads of stars
and white lightning
where Robert Johnson waits
with a handful of brick-dust
and a silver plated revolver
to put a bullet in his head.

But there's a pint of mash
in the glove compartment
and a symphony of cicada
and whippoorwills
to keep the cadence
in his heart clean.
Each stride across the dark assuring,
this will all make a beautiful song someday.

How He Is Not My Child

Sarah Thursday

I didn't stay up at the hospital until three a.m. waiting for the doctors to assess the situation. I didn't have to be the one to sign papers for the insurance company, for permission to treat, for release of legal responsibility. I didn't have to field the calls, protect him from his mother, sit next to him for hours under the cold florescent lights of anger. I did not bear the weight of pen on paper to surrender my flesh and blood to the intervention of complete strangers. I am not the parent deciding always how much to force him to wake up early, get up out of bed, and live his life, or how much to let him sleep, let him fail classes, let him learn from his own mistakes like a boy on the verge of adulthood. I didn't watch the labor of sixteen years calling out from rooftops for men in uniforms to pull him down, dress his wounds, search for more weapons.

P.T.S.D. (Recounting the Streets)

Danielle Mitchell

Isn't your peace that you changed nothing to love him? No routine suffering, cabinet checks, doors locked, checked, unlocked, locked again. He toured the house in semi-circles, twirled your hair counterclockwise & smoked on a perch on the patio chairs high enough to see the night twist inwards. You didn't let him sleep beside you with a bat. Didn't watch us disintegrate into absent need. Or follow his dust. Didn't lay awake with him recounting the streets in Afghanistan—the one he walked down, the hole his foot slipped into where the I.E.D. didn't go off. He was a ghost. Light on his boots. He emptied himself of the house; but he said it would go off. That it would destroy everything & you know by everything he meant that he'd leave the bat & I would need it. You didn't sleep beside it for years. You didn't wake with it lodged deep in my neck.

The apples on this tree

Karie McNeley

remind me how being π'd
from you is so hard to swallow.
Because

sometimes I'd like to be nearer.
An eggplant curled to its stock.
A goose

with its head hung low
in feathers. A barnacle bred
on the

body of a blue whale. Not this
half-rotted fruit. Baked. Powdered
into cake.

We had something fresh-squeezed,
sugar cold & sun-bleached. A million oranges
in a grove.

I want that juice! But I've only two apples.
Us. And for once in my life, cliché
math is aiding me.

Let's start with those two apples. Take one
away. Now we've got one bitter. Me.
Have a bite

of that rancid ship. Swallow it,
port and starboard. Don't end at the bow.
Digest

the sails. Know how many times
I've missed the sandbar with the anchor,
and swooshed

us into the jetty. The juice will drip from
the corner of your lips. I'll taste them, salty.
My opportunity

to regrow into your parasitic paramour
will have branched. You'll no longer be gravid.
I'll spit the seeds

into wet dirt. And nothing will sprout.

Driving By the House I Grew Up In

Ricki Mandeville

I stop at the curb,
wondering if the house remembers
my bare, slender foot creaking
its third stair at midnight
as I sneaked out to meet the boy
with too-long hair, the one Daddy said
was a bad influence,
or Mama's peach pies steaming
on the sill in early afternoon,
or me, safe in bed again by 2 a.m.,
my small transgressions
tucked beneath pink sheets.

Does it remember goodbyes
echoing from the ceiling
to the hardwood floors
as my brother and I went away to college,
leaving our bedrooms hollow until Christmas
or the quadrangle of bright light
cast on the dry summer lawn
from the bathroom window
as I lined my eyes and fluffed my hair,
teetering in 5-inch heels?

Driving away, I sigh and watch it recede
in my rear-view mirror,
crouching like a pale clapboard ghost
among hollies and junipers,
eyes shuttered as though dreaming:
its banisters sleek again
beneath my childish hand.

When the Moon Bleeds

Zack Nelson-Lopiccolo

They said two weeks ago the moon
bled. It looked like a wrinkled old
man with coagulated red
drips from his eyes.

Two weeks ago, I hadn't slept
more than three hours. Awake under
moonlight, computer light,
ignoring the audacity of hues.

Bottles piled in the corner of my room,
ignored like phone calls from
mom, and Stacy. Messages that told
me to look outside, to leave the apartment

for a few hours, get air. Instead
of licking bottles and losing my mind
in a blender memorized books.

They. *They* are all I can think about
the only thing I can write about laying
here naked at noon, drunk, stoned,
with nowhere to go. Except to sleep.

But I can't, every time I close my eyes
I see a bleeding moon, pygmy cut
around a porous belly, drips
dropping into my glass like wine. An entire
work crew of men and women

drilling at grey rock, testing the depths.
I can't sleep knowing I missed a rare
phenomenon, a moon that bled, two
weeks ago. Hidden by reddish clouds,
and I still can't sleep.

Quarter 2:
November, December, January

Everything Overlaps

Daniel McGinn

You fall in love
with someone who knows
the same silence as you,
a silence you share.
They can't see you
so you can't hurt them.

You get sick
of being yourself,
you have to learn
to forgive
yourself first
for whatever the hell
it was you did
that made things
turn out like this.

And you've got to
forgive them too.
It's not so much
anger now,
you can understand
how a person might
grow tired of you.

Maybe you go
to the doctor because
your feet hurt
and you cry so hard
you can hardly
see for days
after you encounter
the person
who abandoned you.

A letter arrives
addressed to you
with layers
of frustrated tape
pressed to the seal.

Maybe you are just a dog
after your own tail.
Maybe you thought
you were done looking back
at shadows;

they come to your door
like snow clouds.
You open the door,
it's cold outside,
but you stand there
waiting to see
what is going
to happen,

because you've
lived in this town
all of your life
it's never snowed here,
not once.

Long Beach Parrots

Tamara Madison

In Long Beach the parrots chatter,
winging from palm to palm
in the dry sky. Sun lashes the fronds.

The green birds have bred out
their reds and yellows; they fly,
noisy, in flocks of jade. These

are not the birds that live on porches
in cages and practice human speech;
they have no memory of the Amazon.

These birds speak the wordless
cacophony of traffic, navigate
the sunny jungle of broad streets, palms,
eucalyptus, conversing together in bleats.

We speak our thoughts in language
that bears a long, long memory; theirs
is the lucky language of Now.

In the Ballcrawl

J.D. Isip

The best years of my life I spent a rat
Hired for three summers to be Chuck E. Cheese
After the second time I applied
After my friend, Cody, put in a good word—
Cody is white.
I slipped into a matted gray body suit.

The best years of my life I spent a rat
Happy to token my group, happy to Franklin
Our Peanuts gang on campus
And in all the pictures
I was never white.
The suit always smelled like the last Chuck E.

The best years of my life I spent a rat
Cody was my best friend and I hated him
So much that I wanted nothing more
Than to be him.
Outside fluff, inside the ripe sweat of hours.

The best years of my life I spent a rat
Ratting along the intricate
Labyrinthine tunnelry of angst
And rat rage.
I wore a hollow head.

The best years of my life I spent a rat
Watching him through eyes
Of rude-cut metal mesh
Scraping my inner face raw.
Giant rat hands that felt nothing...

The best years of my life I spent a rat
Capable of scrounging up
A meal, but happy to leftover,
Crumb, swallow up –
Shuck and jive in the ballcrawl.

threeway with arturo bandini and camilla lombard

Christian Lozada

i, like her, didn't care for him at first
with his stained wife beater and orange fingers
he was kind of a whiney dick
but i recognized his smell
his boundless desire
i, too with family in the east, wanted this city
to open up to me
and she, like me, wanted this first-stop-in-the-U.S. city
to embrace her

his smell, that too desperate smell,
lingered and his racism pulled me in
because i knew and hated huaraches
just like i knew and hated my brown skin
and my last name that ends with a soft vowel
we shared that hate for being neither fish nor fowl
and love for man and beast alike

camilla lopez
became our shared mayan princess
she who hated her huaraches
and brown skin

part of me was glad that the brown, harsh desert
swallowed his note to Camilla
because his heartbreak meant
i touched a piece of her he could not
because his heartbreak meant
he obviously learned nothing from us

A Tragedy of Birds

John Brantingham

1.
Five years old almost,
out behind the farthest raspberry bush
in the backyard,
against the chain link fence
but cross legged,
and drowsed in the late August heat,
teaching myself physics by flexing
and unflexing the dead crow's wing,
stretching it father each time
until it snaps off in my hand.
When it cracks, a spume of dust
forms itself into the shape of a kidney.
Little mites crawl on my hand.

2.
Thirteen years old with a pellet pistol
and in front of friends.
I draw on the bird above me in a 17th century
duelling pose and fire, hitting the thing.
We watch it tumble out of the air
and onto the neighbor's front lawn.
My buddy says "one shot"
with a kind of awe because we'd watched
The Deer Hunter on tape the day before.

3.
Twenty-five years old just married
and cooking a chicken for my wife.
I make the thing dance like
it's in the "Sledgehammer" video.
Blood runs thinly down my hands
and arms until my wife laughs,
and I clean it off with hot water
and lots of soap.
We're not going out tonight.

We have our first tiny apartment
with an atrium in the middle of it
and in the evening we'll turn off the lights
and watch wild parrots that roost
on the slats on the top of the atrium,
squawking their complaints to each other
about being taken from their jungle home
and put in cages until their people
have grown tired of them
and then let them out in this world to fight
for themselves in whatever flocks they can form.
They tell each other
about their first homes
and what life was like when they were young.
They squawk about being fledglings.
They squawk about feeling so alone.

Retreat

Marianne Stewart

I caved to
To my 3AM impulse
And flattened my belly
Into 10th street
Propped up my chin
On the smooth and reflective
Yellow line
Comforted,
My fingers in the deep cracks
Of the asphalt.
This is my church sometimes
This is my most sacred only holy
Existing in the drips
All melodramatic
And secret
And embarrassingly self aware
At least enough
To know rolling around in the street leads to
Glass in the hair
But startled skittish
When beady eyes and hunkered spine
Crawled out of the drain
Those tiny hands
I was up and running
Faster than headlights
Living is ridiculous
Cars alarming
Raccoons the worst.

The Catwalk

Nancy Lynée Woo

The reason why I don't clean
or fix my car, and then drive
around Belmont Shore looking
smug with taillights smashed
and duct tape mirrors gaping
at the fluffed white people
shopping is because I might want
them to be offended by my
poorness. I learned this in
4th grade when I would, without
fail, walk into my Gifted And
Talented Education classroom—
where smart kids go to be told
they're smart—in Orange County—
where the envious go to flourish
in their hive cement sidewalks—
15 minutes late every day, creaking
open the door to teacher already
talking, interrupting, because
my mother, worn out and coffee-fixed,
could never fit a schedule,
it was her subtle way of resisting
her tug-a-long fate—at least she could
rebel against time—and usually
my clothes were dirty or old or
hand-me-downs friends' mothers
who pitied me gave me, and here
I learned how to walk in this rag
fashion show kind of way, quiet but
smiling that smile like I was saying
yeah, look at me, look at the isness
of my difference, I'll strut on in
when I want and grin until
you believe I am grinning, smirk
wide like I am better than you for
knowing what poverty feels like.

Credo

Donna Hilbert

I believe in the Tuesdays
and Wednesdays of life,
the tuna sandwich lunches
and TV after dinner.
I believe in coffee with hot milk
and peanut butter toast,
Rosé wine in summer
and Burgundy in winter.

I am not in love with holidays,
birthdays—nothing special—
and weekends are just days
numbered six and seven,
though my love
dozing over TV golf
while I work the Sunday puzzle
might be all I need of life
and all I ask of heaven.

Ceremony

Ricki Mandeville

I return you to air, free you to wind,
the light, pure powder of you scattered,
gliding west on slipstreams of cormorants.
The silk dust of your bones.

The light, pure powder of you scattered
on a red altar of clouds.
The silk dust of your bones
a delicate stain against the sky.

On a red altar of clouds,
the solemn litany of sunset,
a delicate stain against the sky.
The sea chanting in Latin voices.

The solemn litany of sunset:
salt to ashes, ashes to salt.
The sea, chanting in Latin voices
as waves reach to gather you.

Salt to ashes, ashes to salt.
You are a fine smoke on the water
as waves reach to gather you,
a pale film on my hands.

You are a fine smoke on the water,
settling, drifting,
a pale film on my hands
as I dust you toward home.

Settling, drifting,
you glide west on slipstreams of cormorants
as I dust you toward home,
returning you to air, freeing you to wind.

Clenched Fists

Clint Margrave

I'm thinking of the way we're born with our fists clenched
and how we die with them open.
So much in life depends on
these two simple gestures.
I'm thinking of our hands
and all the ways we use them.
The way we grasp for things.
The way we run our fingers down each other's backs.
The way we show affection,
give pleasure with them,
bring ourselves and others to the point of orgasm.
The way we pick up a pen
and write things down with them.
The way they shake sometimes.
The way we build bridges,
or slip rings onto the fingers
of those we love.
The way they can be used for terrible things,
like strangling somebody
or slapping someone's face.
The way we hold guns with them, light fires,
fly airplanes into buildings.
The way we can pin somebody down against their will
or hold them back from error.
The way we use them to feed ourselves.
The way we steal with them.
The way we hold them up to protect our faces,
or use them to cover our mouths.
The way we make sound.
The way we snap.
The way we take measurements.
The way we raise them over our heads.
Put gloves on to keep them warm
or to knock each other out.

The way we can somehow map our destinies across them,
or lift ourselves up,
or cut things down,
or hold on tightly to things.
The way we can let them go.

Waiting on Winter

JL Martindale

The dead yard begs for a shampoo of rain.
Our red brick patio, bleached, gasps for shade.
You and I sit sweaty, sucking ice cubes
that taste like yellow onions you froze and I forgot.

In front of the twenty dollar fan, I dream past Octobers
cool enough for pumpkin pie and hot cider. I don't even like apple cider.
Dear, you say, *we're running out of ice.*

The cats sprawled on bathroom tile, look at me, accusingly.
I'm sorry, I say to them, to you, to no one. I *am* sorry.
We said we'd build from this, take this house and make it home
It was supposed to bring us together.

But instead, we sit opposite each other, seething, sucking ice.
Maybe it will be better when snow falls on acrylic landscapes
that hang over headboard horizons.

Plum

Shannon Phillips

I stood in the break room with him while
he rambled on about flight reservations and
accrued vacation hours.

It was like waiting for water to still,
for the image to stop rippling,
for when I could finally focus.

The membrane of his lip was so delicate
I almost expected to catch a tiny flutter of a pulse
like at the dip in the bone where his throat
merged with his pectoral plate.

His lower lip in particular
such a ripened grape,
that if I barely made a tiny slice
with perhaps, say,
an Exacto knife:

It would burst.

A couple of coworkers everyone speculated were sleeping together
returned from a smoke break.

"Hey, do you want this plum?"
He was cleaning out his lunch box;
I'm sure he'd hate to throw away something
that was still good.

I plucked it from him,
wrapped it in a paper towel to keep it from getting marred,
and stashed it in my purse.

What a man needed a mouth like that for, I don't know.

Your Mother Laughing

Daniel McGinn

Stand at the sink.
Pull strawberry after strawberry from a green basket.
Cut them with a butter knife.
Whose hands are these?
The fingers look like your mothers.
One hand slowly pats the other. Sigh.
Look out the window at the same empty street.

Look at these sundae cups that were stored
in a box in the garage. You like them.
You never saw them before she died.
You stand in her kitchen and wish you could ask her
where she got these. These thick glass cups
must have belonged to your Grandmother.
They're so goddamned beautiful
they almost make you cry.

Sprinkle sugar on strawberries in a bowl.
Go to the freezer, get the ice cream
with bits of vanilla bean in it.
Roll it into the scoop your mother owned.
It belongs in your hand.

Summer strawberries make ice cream pink.
They taste terrific.
You eat dessert in front of a television
in the house you grew up in.
You sit in the dark watching *The Munsters*.
Something funny happens and your mother starts to laugh.

Seeking Snowstorms

Sergei A. Smirnoff

this train has been traveling east
200 hundred kilometers an hour

i ponder it going the wrong way
gaze out my window to make sure

i've been hiding behind my camera
veronica doesn't like to smile

there is nothing else worth
taking a picture of

i've seen all these withering fields
and rotting cities before

two time zones behind us
the laborers watched us pass by

Sacrament

Athena

Baptism
It looked exactly
as it does
in the movies
Yellow sun
falling back
Green cloudy water
folding her body
in two
A trail
of tiny bubbles
marching
to the surface
Push off
Reach up!
she heard
the voices say
Then
cold air
on panicked fingers
sweet air
in grateful lungs
A baptism
on the Little Spokane

Extreme Unction
And all she could think was
this is what it feels like
Drowning
with your loved ones
floating down river
steering their boats
with surprising dexterity
And it was you all the time
it was you
playing ding dong ditch
with death

He smiles this time
shallowing the waters
stilling the moment
shutting the door
behind frightened footsteps
waiting
waiting for when it feels
more satisfying
to bring you home

Against the Weeds

Fernando Gallegos

Woven across multiple layers
I can't remove myself
Intertwined heart
Veins
Blood with dirt
Roots reaching for water
My eyes searching for light
The flesh feels the sun
Hair full of leaves
Fall, spring, summer
Exist at once
I'm nourished by the refuse
But I still hunger for life
Hours, days
I flower, try to reach you
grab your attention
Voiceless for so long
I dig myself deeper
I can't escape
Bones become brittle
against the stones, rocks, dirt
The mind is lost
Against the weeds

17th Street

Kevin Ridgeway

She bakes the French bread
In the backroom
Smoking half a cigarette
Underneath the 3 am moonlight
The back door ajar
Massaging her hair
Underneath her employee cap
Adjusting her upside down badge

8am rolls around in a stupor
And she announces this French bread
Is on sale into a stale old PA microphone
With a genius for wordplay
And a savvy for sales

3PM rolls along like the
Morning didn't exist
And she pulls onto 17th street
With a wedding cake in her trunk
Up to the winding hills
Of Anaheim,
Searching for the stray balloons

6PM approaches, time to
Start counting endless
Receipts and quirky scribbling
On them to make the bank
For the dozens upon dozens
Of goods sold that day

She comes home for me to
Massage her neck, falling
Asleep with a lit cigarette
In her mouth
I put it out.

When My Mother Danced

Denise R. Weuve

My father left for the weekend.
This time to Seattle,
and as usual she had pressed
his cotton blue shirt and put
a perfect crease in his work jeans.
It was too neat
for a man who would spend the entire
time behind the wheel.
My grandmother came over
from the community center
where she had played Bingo,
and was the proud winner
of four Farmer John's chickens,
and three pounds of extra lean ground meat.
To celebrate, my mother
went over to the pop top stereo
removed the plastic doily,
and selected an outdated 8-track.
She danced with my Grandmother
dipping her, and turning her
as if she were a music box ballerina,
the way my father would have
with her, if he was ever around.
But they were two women
who did not need permission
to pin their paisley dresses
above their knees, whisper
curse words, or dance in each other's arms.
They put the coffee table up on the sofa
and showed off the Sugar Foot,
Twisted until they wore holes
through the carpet, then Two-Stepped
to Eddie Rabbit's "Traveling man."

Shiva for the Stars

Jessica Claire Bennish

I like the taste of night.
The way it bites all sharp.
Air teasing.
just so,
Go to the desert, sit shivah for the stars.
Like a wake. You know.
Pretend to swallow the moon,
maybe you will become pregnant
and shoot moonbeams from
somewhere.
Who am I to say.

you sit shivah for the stars a thousand times over
and remember their lives even though you were
not there to see them, because they are dead
a thousand times over yet still shine bright.

Stellar Murder

Clifton Snider

From what I'm told
the tiniest particle
in my living cells
resembles the architecture
of the universe;
a swooping image of bright orange & red
against solid black
generated by a computer
illustrates a black hole
two billion years ago
slowly sucking in a dying star
caught
too close to the hungry hole
caught
in a tidal disruption–
only
there is no moon,
no tide going out,
only the bleak darkness
of a galaxy
found in space
and a star
that is no more.

The Virgin Electric

Alisha Attella

The Virgin processes down
the street on her half shell of
chicken wire and novena candles
leading a dance with the sun
glinting off her glass blue veil.

The children follow her with swaying
bodies and drum beats and sweat.
They're ecstatic with her mother bear love,
waiting to hear what she'll tell dad about the
broken glasses and four letter words
and chicken head rituals at midnight.

She stands also, home in the yard
at our old Cape house
all electric with the cast-offs
from high tension wires;
flanked, guarded by weather
rotten post beams
and the prayer flag underwear
that flicks on the clothesline.

We sit there in that drone womb
venerating her sandblasted brow
and lighting citronella candles
from wirechair pews.
Waiting, poised with our
wine glasses and five dollar words
and long, deep talks at midnight.

Waiting, for ecstasy or mother love
or the sun to come from behind
the cool autumn clouds and flood
us in its glass-blue intercession.

The Struggle to Stay the Same

Olivia Somes

Tangerine decorative scarves, nicks of magazines,
in the hospital room, you made everything you:
a poster of George Michael's torn jeans,
the Dollywood snow globe you picked up
at a yard sale outside a donut shop, next to you,
white specks jumble to the break beat of life support.
You say *we're going to make a party out of all of this,*
I can barely feel my knees. I keep smiling along
even when you choke up blood on a noise maker,
as you talk of your sister's wedding: we danced
to Bon Jovi telling us to live on a pray,
your Uncle slopping some story about
a sledgehammer in Newark and a dead ex-con,
boys wrecked on beer, spitting over the pier.
You refused the best man *he smiles like
a dragon, breath like sardines,* he looked alright to me.
That was you, seeing deep into the foil of things.

You knew I would change, you made me promise not to,
the hair went, that was easy you wore wigs anyways,
a pink perm for a rainy day, Cleopatra's flat black cut,
when your frame made a ghost of you, it was bearable,
costumes you wore like Halloween was once a week,
today I am John Keats, blood flaked on your teeth,
it's not funny, I laugh. You dressed up like James Dean
one New Year's Eve, jumping on the bar table
anyone want a joyride, unlit cigarette in your mouth
joking up the death of the young and famous,
you saw me, meek in a crème sweater, a knee long skirt,
you pulled me along in front of you through
Smoke trails, peanut shells, an old lady with a poodle.

I want to be pulled into the front of this,
This show of the way we were, in this room,
us reminiscing over the sand castle war with
your brother when we were ten, the gnome
collection you acquired from random front lawns,

you don't have arms anymore as you tell a story,
you just barrel along the shave pear of a face,
the bald, bulge wrist bone chumming with us,
the skeleton of you becoming my friend too.
All I want to do is crumble on top of waxed floor,
complain about the smell of the hospital,
get mad over the food, the pain you pretend you're not in,
talk about the others dying around us, about you.
I just sit here laughing as you struggle not to pass out.

Resurrección

Zack Nelson-Lopiccolo

Jesus works at the tacos y mariscos
place two blocks from my cramped
studio. I usually speak to him in Spanish
because his English is still broken up
like tequila bottles in the alley.

He'd gotten mixed up in some drug
dealing in his hometown (Nuevo Laredo)
and came here to reset.

It's been three years. He's always
working just to keep enough food
in the fridge and make rent
in his cardboard apartment.

I toss him an extra tip when
I've got it. We're friends, *amigos*, both
know how life can beat you with a bat
and then push you in front of traffic.

His hours make it hard for him to get
his papers. His boss won't give him a damn
day off. I got him the forms and he's filled
them out. They're sitting collecting dust
like comets crossing a cold universe, alone.

Tape Deck Blues

Kevin Ridgeway

I could not afford CDs growing up
and had to listen to my brother's
old cassette tapes,
the Pixies and the Beatles and Nirvana
roaring out of a paint stained boom box
as I paced back and forth dreaming
of CDs and girls clad in only my silk Gucci
dress shirts dancing with me
to "I Wanna Sex You Up"
just like in those R&B videos I used to watch
I was king of the world in my imagination
but I had to make sure I had plenty of pencils
when the cassette tapes got eaten inside
the tape deck, and the second hand store t-shirts
I wore with their stains did not impress any
of the girls at school who listened to Blink-182
and Limp Bizkit and all of those
other strange bands
and they did not want to sex me up.

Interview with Sister [age 44]

Danielle Mitchell

Who am I without you & the open-heart system of your dining room table? The daughters gathered there, little birds in their breasts all fluttering & wide mouthed. Teach me your lessons from the vacuum. In the absence of our mother you are my mother. In your memory I'm always a woman. A little reflection of yourself come early. Before the girls began to grow inside you & we planted the willow in the backyard beside your pond to remind you of our grandmother—& now those girls, long & weepy, sprout in their new bodies by the pool. Where did your longing go? When did you know that your young sister was full of wings & light & forgetting the absence she needed you for. Laid in the yard, wanting to be in your image to nest & go & the kitchen & the side yard where the muse keeps caged always at least one beautiful bird of prey. Why are you always so busy? How do you keep the days as they tumble out from clogging at your feet? Like prayers. Like groceries. What are we if not the answer to the other.

Bone-Yard Romance

Larry Duncan
To S.L.

We were young.
I swear.

Your hair like gauze,
frayed and flaxen
in the harsh halo
of the porch light.

It was an anniversary
or your cousin's birthday
and I danced with your mother
as your father watched
through the spindles
of the porch he'd built,
his eyes like steel diamonds,
his dog biting at the coils
of his cage set back
along the skeletal range
of September trees.

And you were beautiful,
you were always beautiful
with your pock marked skin
and your frail fingers
and the way you laughed
like forever,
like the echo of a wooden bat against a sheet metal sign.

The last time I saw you
you kept losing track
mid-sentence,
staring off to the treeline
where the Rottweiler was caged.

You said it was because of the pills
or the blow,
your head leading the way
when you struck the other cars
crossing the intersection.

There were pink,
ragged scars
up and down your limbs
from where the asphalt ate your skin
and the shards of fiberglass
had torn,
like chromatic teeth,
down to the bone.

We had this idea—
Kerouac and Cassidy
on the cover of a Penguin Classic
their hands in their pockets
smirking at the camera
young and beautiful forever,
and Ginsberg on a stage
visible only
through the rents
of cigarette smoke
and waving hands,
the bottle passing,
his body contorted
to form a some kind of sign
and everyone crying "holy, holy, holy!"

We wanted to be holy.
We wanted beaten down and holy, too.

Only we didn't know the rest of it, '
that there were cars crossing the intersection

the Long days in between
calling us to the kiss and scream of metal,
to the ragged shapes of blood colored glass
strewn around the wreckage.

We were drawn into the rhythm
Of "angelheaded hipsters burning for the ancient heavenly connection to
the starry dynamo in the machinery of night",
of angels burning so hard and so fast that they simply exploded into light.
Here.
Flash.
Gone.

Lifted up and scattered like so much stardust.

But not the rest of it.
Not Jack bent over the toilet vomiting blood,
crying through the torrent of alcohol induced hemorrhages
not "Holy!" but "Help me!"
"Help me, Stella, I'm bleeding."
Not Neal, his last bit of potential burned
out on a few beautiful letters,
staggering off from a wedding party
in a Seconal haze
to die in the wet dark
like a wounded animal,
like a dog.

"Against the ruin of the world there is only one defense—the creative act."

Kenneth Rexroth wrote that.
You were always trying to get me to read Rexroth.
And I did.
And I believe that.
It might be the only thing I believe.

Like faith.

Since I read that line I've been repeating it.

Like a mantra.

(Holy! Holy! Holy!...)

And now you're gone
and I'm still here.
36
and half a bottle of whiskey
and half a pack of cigarettes
and the next day like a pebble in the hand.

There are no anniversaries anymore
no days to mark
nothing but the dog
and his cage
his face hanging
like a Daikjin
Mask amid the chains.

And I hear him
like a voice
some other chant
voice like smoke
teeth like grates
on the oven

And I think of all those years
caught in that ridiculous pose,
too drunk to write,
too caught up in my own beatific gaze
to hear the hounds,
to feel the heat of the furnace wall.

Always running,
                    running,
running.

And for what?
Towards what?

Three DUI's in three states,
a possession charge,
a broken marriage and half-a-dozen broken relationships besides,
and not even a handful of beautiful letters to show for it.

I see you now—
as you were
and as you are—
Saint Veronica of the Vera Icon
imposed on the shroud of my sight
and I watch the clock
and I count my coughs,
and I forgo sleep,
not to howl mad at the moon,
but to pound the keys,
to catch up to the clock.

Especially on nights like tonight,
when the house is asleep
and it's cold enough to make parts of me ache
and there's so much work to be done
and it feels so very, very late.

Westminster Abbey, March 1991

John Brantingham

I got my first migraine staring at Chaucer's grave in Westminster Abbey. It was a real migraine, complete with an aura that nearly blinded me, and I had nausea and the rest. I was twenty and living away from home for the first time, and the migraine probably had to do with too much excitement, too much beer and too little water, or a food allergy, or I don't know what, but I didn't know what a migraine was then, so I thought I was having a spiritual moment with old Geoffrey – that he was communing with me, and it felt significant. It seems ridiculous now thinking back, but it made a sort of sense at the time. Life was different in those months. Everything was different. I had fallen in love and found the British reading room and met people from all over – people who had done things like scampering over the Berlin Wall or hitchhiking across Asia – and every night we drank and talked and read and lived. There are times in life when you read the right book at just the right time or meet the right person who understands you or travel some place that silences you for one long lost breath, and you get it, and you understand for the first time, and all of those things were happening to me, all of those celestial events were going on for me in London right then. It was that moment that I got my first migraine, so maybe it's not so strange that I felt like Chaucer was reaching out to me from wherever he was and blessing me and telling me that what I was doing right now was in some way sacred.

Tattoo

Thomas R. Thomas

standing naked
in the shower
she scrubs
the tattoo
just above
her breast

the wrinkles
distort the
flower of
her youth

and soap
won't remove
the wrinkled
image

Winter Moon Pantoum

Ricki Mandeville

Outside, a scarf of light around a throat of moon,
a wind slipping a veil of clouds around the stars,
and I'm a silhouette behind a frosted windowpane,
craving the silent benediction of snow.

A wind slipping a veil of clouds around the stars;
steep hillsides buried deep in fallen leaves
craving the silent benediction of snow
beneath an orchestra of tossing trees.   .

Steep hillsides buried deep in fallen leaves,
strange shadows turning in an endless dance
beneath an orchestra of tossing trees,
and here, on the window ledge, his books all stacked.

Strange shadows turning in an endless dance
against my walls, moon-paled to silver gray,
and here, on the window ledge, his books all stacked
dreaming the touch of his long, brown hands.

Against my walls, moon-paled to silver gray,
my shadow waltzes in a flannel gown,
dreaming the touch of his long, brown hands
as clocks strike winter in the hall.

My shadow waltzes in a flannel gown,
and I'm a silhouette behind a frosted windowpane
as clocks strike winter in the hall.
Outside, a scarf of light around a throat of moon.

Eating

Shannon Phillips

I've always admired peanut butter
for its adhering qualities.

And the apple for enduring despite the bad
rap it received as the forbidden fruit.

And bananas for preserving their dignity
even after Freud.

And the pomegranate for conspiring with
Hades to trap Persephone.

And tomatoes for maintaining a binary
identity in the Fruit-n-Veggie universe.

Berries and grapes also have their virtues
except they often get made into spread,

relinquishing their identity, their form.
That's about as good as a woman

who melts in a man's arms,
oozing through his fingers,

nothing to grasp, no tangible resistance,
no satisfying pierce and chomp for the teeth.

That's another reason to admire peanut butter:
Because it puts up with jelly.

All The Ways I Deserve You (Long Beach)

Sarah Thursday

I was excited to meet you.
You would be more like me.
All those years being yanked
from one place to the next,
being pulled out of school early
means I wasn't coming back.
I can't remember the names
of my teachers, but I can recite
cities like family members.

Then I met you, Long Beach,
the city of everything,
of Cambodia and Mexico,
of apartments spilling bodies
in the streets, spilling ranchero melodies
and clicking tongues full of Vietnam.
My color was a minority.
My clothes from donated boxes
did not flinch you—
you with your narrow alleyways
and grubby-cheeked children.

I was at home before I knew
how long I'd stay. I knew you
were like me, born of struggle
and sitting on window sills staring
out at distant city lights.

Even when we got a new father
and lived among your riverside homes,
it was all wrong like me.
Concrete banks dressed in graffiti.
Wilderness trails where teenage boys
played war around stained mattresses
left by public refugees.

I became a woman in your sunlight.
I never had to deserve you.

You knew all my names,
even when I left you.
I tried to be the golden boardwalks
of Hermosa and Redondo
but they pushed me out
to the gum-stained sidewalks
of Lawndale, where train tracks
drew lines between me and him,
where girls like me paid their own way
through city college.

Then he left me for Westwood,
a place I could never see
my own stark reflection,
so I came home to you,
and the best skin of you.

I wore my new clothes here
on all your borders north
and south, and east and west.
All your contradictions sang
like love songs, even when for years
I was only your mistress.

Other cities have soccer moms
and radio-friendly punk rock,
winter tans and French manicures,
but I know, even they find a place
in your diagonals, your Wardlows
that cross both apartment projects
and gated communities.

I will grow old here, far from your shore.
Even though I bought a house
next to the tracks again, your tracks
comfort me—not division but connection,
a literal line of how close we are,
side-by-side, lying in the lap of you.

Quarter 3:
February, March, April

After the Break Up

Raquel Reyes-Lopez

I walk nude. Breasts bounce.
Nipples perk from chill.
I close the door behind.
Open tattered shower curtains.

I pull up from inside the drain
hairs. The only thing you left
behind. I slap them against the wall.

You tossed my love into the sewer
as easy as your bowels push shit.

I can only wonder
if I grab a wire hanger
use your hairs as bait
fish within the drain
could I reel
my heart
back in?

Dinner Date

Daniel McGinn

She wishes she was small like a child's blouse.
She wishes it was pink.
She is trying to eat in little bites.
There are white tablecloths and couples at other tables.
She does not like the way I look at her mouth
every time she opens it. She is eating as little as possible.
Eating is loaded with facial expressions and noises.
She won't risk either. I am cutting and cutting my steak,
knife and fork, knife and fork, grabbing dinner
by the horns and wrestling it down. She sits demurely,
trying to listen. She would say something
but I am doing the talking, effortlessly saying
all the wrong things.
The blood is warm and pulsing in her cheeks.
She is forgetting how to blink.
She tries a forkful of salad and a spring leaf slides
out of the bowl, the vinegar and oil seep
into the white table cloth. She watches the stain grow.
My steak is bleeding profusely.
The trout on her plate was fried with head and tail intact.
She has no idea what to do with this eyeless fish;
she doesn't want to rip out its spine or cut off its head.
Not on the first date. She is uncertain what to do
so she sits there doing nothing. The only thing she knows
is she's not going to kiss me. Not after watching me eat.

"Love" Vs. "In Love"

G. Murray Thomas

In love is wanting.
Love is giving.
In love is, "I want it now!"
Love is, "I can wait."

In love is, if you don't smile at me,
    or you smile in the wrong way,
    it'll ruin my day.

Love is, if you're not smiling,
    I want to make you smile.

In love is dying when you don't call,
    but not making the call myself because
    it takes no effort to answer the phone,
    and I need you to make the effort.

Love is calling just to hear your voice.

In love is worrying when I'm not there,
    afraid of the fun you might be having without me.

Love is wishing I was there,
    but if I'm not,
    hoping you are having fun without me.

In love is obsessing on what comes next,
    always feeling it could be more,
    or longer,
    or sweeter,
    somehow better.

Love is savoring every moment.

In love is a hole,
    which needs to be filled.

Love is a fountain.

In love is desperate.
Love is relaxed.

In love is I, me, mine.
Love is you,
    always you.

Single Women's Rehabilitation Day

Danielle Mitchell

Think of me as light, imperishable. Think small,
think stubborn bean of a light on & ongoing toward
whatever, whatever is out there. An island,
or a morning. Maybe it's a boat; I don't know.
I am that light.

Today the doctor said if I go in the sun I'll get a rash.
She didn't say if that was the exposed skin or
if my whole body would be covered by daylight
& I didn't ask. For the first time in weeks
I wanted to go outside. Wanted to interrogate
my face with sun or cloud. Things are finally starting
to turn around, I thought. If we could all
repeat it like this: *I am*

imperfect, I am imperfect, I am imperfect but I know
how to dance. Let that be the journey's new slogan.
On the open range it will be harder to contain
my anxiety. I'll take fewer medicines. You will call me
a lark & my eyes will show their light at the seams.
We will cry into each other. We will circle the wagons
build the grandest campfire & let everything breathe.
We will make a day of it we'll call it Single Women's
Rehabilitation Day, call it that

& laugh as if all I need is a man. I tell you I am a light.
Come to me on the river; we'll shove ourselves into
the water's smoky path. Whenever you're drowning,
remember—let someone down, let someone down
so hard you come back up more yourself. That rarity.
That luminosity. That is you, we sail to at night.

Cult of Chili Thursday

Manuel Gutierrez

House: a dog blind in one eye
dusty dry air stings my nose
we sit reminiscing while
Mitchell at his laptop shouts "Soraka
my Soraka".

Park: a jungle gym we climb in the dark
with sandy socks like we're children
again and Salty talks about getting cruised
by horny men on PCH during night walks.
I fake a smile and pretend I can relate

Buffet: if someone doesn't eat the cheesy nanners
or the ketchup covered rice crispy
we won't get a ride back.
Dayday calls it disgusting cafeteria food
after eating four plates

Ghetto streets: Salty talks about the bums
giving each other head in back of the McDonald's.

Couch: we brainstorm
and he won't stop bitching
unless his card idea "Booberella"
gets made. Not going to happen.
He never stops bringing it up.

Car: Hans tells me if I were a real friend
I'd kill him without raping the body.
I make the promise.

Tom's: everyone gathers for Chili Thursday
religiously. We all have five dollars
saved; large chili cheese fries, Dr. Pepper.
Everyone knows their chair.
It's not the chili that matters.

Snappy Refrigerator Magnet Sayings #1

Nancy Lynée Woo

I like my men how I like my
crossed word puzzles:
complex, frustrating and
nongiveupable –

The only love worth having
labyrinthine.

I am no princess hoping on toads;
Give me your ugly, your worst,
your most frightening Minotaur
and a string.

photo I should've taken

Shannon Phillips

The lime square of his swim shorts
grows smaller and faster

as his bare feet launch
mini-comet tails of sand
behind him.

I catch
his smile, all gleaming teeth and glee,
flashing back at
his dad, a man in pursuit.

If I Owned A Suit

Elder Zamora
for Scott Creley

If I owned a suit,
I might have worn it to read this poem.

I might have stayed up late into the night pressing it,
going over every inch with a roller to make
sure that the lint from my aging carpet did no
discredit to the fine Men's Warehouse Construction.

I might have laid it out on my bed, a flat version of myself on which I
I could overlay different colored shirts and neckties to put together
various two dimensional me's who could attend functions and drink
cocktails and talk to other people in suits about suit things
like finances and elections and just what the US should do
with that one country with all the problems.

I might have at some point panicked because I would soon realize that
A. I don't know how to make a necktie, and that
B. I'm nowhere near hip enough or sleazy enough to wear a suit without
one.

I might have realized that my one friend who does know how
and who used to make the knots for the rest of us before job
interviews and weddings, my friend Sepehr, lives in North Carolina now, and
he's married, and he's got a real job, and he wouldn't like it
if I called at 2 or 3 to ask for step by step instructions on how to make
a half-Windsor knot. He would instead yell,
and ask me why I even own a suit anyway?

I might have sat up the rest of the night reflecting on that,
why a suit? Why does it matter if a jacket and a pair of trousers match, and
are tailored in such a way that some rich Frenchman or Englishman
or Ralph Lauren or whoever designs the suits they sell at outlets would
deem fashionable
and acceptable.

I might have not been able to let that go, so that today
I might have shown up with that suit, all balled up and torn
and doused in kerosene, for a grand statement on what I think of
complacency
and fashion and the yoke of societal norms we all wear, and with a cloud of
black smoke this evening would have taken a very different turn.

But I don't own a suit. Not one.
So instead last night I watched the last season of Battlestar Galactica,
and got a good
night's sleep, and that show is fantastic.

The Ripening

Tobi Cogswell

It is summer. You are fifty
going on twenty, she is your girl
next door. She invents the words
you want to say, laughs
as she climbs a tree, dares you
to come get her, move in
close and hold her—

her hair wild like blackberry brambles
offering themselves and their fruit,
her kiss sweet as tea.
Wild and sweet, bare knees
and skinned elbows, she reaches
her arms around your neck, pulls
you toward her.

That secret place—you go back
again and again.
That luminous wind
and the mockingbird.
Your voice. Her voice.

The Rose that Lupe

Tamara Madison

The rose that Lupe
gave me perches all day
on my desk, in the lip
of my blue commuter cup
for I have no vase to put it in

It wilts through "le jour et la date,"
the conjugations of *aller*
and the English class admonitions
to *Shut the mouths up*
and G*et your face back
in your seat.* And every time

I rest at my desk
its deep and worldly sweetness
reminds me of the gardens outside
where hunched *abuelitas*
and retired longshoremen
proudly tend their flower beds.

I don't think they would mind
that a young girl
not yet worldly
has plucked one in its prime
and given it to her teacher
who then, day-battered,
brings it home
and places it in a half-inch
of water in a wineglass

where its petals smash
against the glass, look
like a flamenco dancer's
cast-off magenta skirt
and smell like everyone's idea
of earthly love.

neurosity XII
i was going to kill my heroine

Jax NTP

but changed my mind — *you cannot find peace by avoiding life.* everyone must wrestlealone in the dark — *this is what we do.* this is what people do. *they stay alive for each other.*

he's a business man of some sort, a failed novelist, lacking voice, now only writes obituaries for the town's newspaper. he met her on the freezing beach in Montauk, many many februaries ago. when she asked him for the last piece of bread, then ate it right out of his hand before he could even answer — an act so intimate as if they were already lovers.

and years after they married, she still likes to buy her own flowers — to throw her own parties (a mask of confidence), but he knows: she's always throwing parties to cover up the silence. to this day, she harbors the same thought as she did while growing up: *the thought that if she allowed the silence to persist for too long, somehow she would disappear.*

now, she hates it when he gives her that look. a look that says hosting parties is so trivial — that she is trivial. yet in her triviality, he's addicted to her pain. she is lovable, thus, completely un-leave-able, he finds comfort in her misery — such comfort that it causes him to stray away from her truth: the fact that she wrestles alone in the dark, living, living only to satisfy, only to satisfy him.

Beautiful

JL Martindale

I did it after he said,
"I guess you're kinda cute,
but not pretty, and in no way beautiful."
It'd be the last time I let him play The Cure
and spread the tiger blanket
in front of that giant mirror
leaning against the wall.
I offered myself, like a good girl,
then purged violent urges
against his perfectly freckled nudity
fantasizing
about shattering
that fucking glass
into his face, scarring those eyes
watching himself
penetrate
               me.
Detached
like strangers,
I posed for him
like the girls in the porno
playing on that tiny TV
in the thrift store on Hollywood.
On cue, I shivered and shook.
Cried out my release
before he lost his.
Smiled while he claimed
he felt everything.
Knowing
he'd realize
only after I'd gone:
my purse heavy
with his beloved bootleg CD
of Nine Inch Nails'
demo tracks,

the one I gave him
when I thought
he thought
I was pretty.

What Is Broken

Kevin Clothier

A china cup from your Mother's collection
fell on the floor this morning.
One careless swipe of the duster
and a world held in memory
shattered at your feet.

So you scooped up pieces,
colored gold, ivory, azure, and rose,
wrapped them in a dish towel
and smashed them
against the porch steps.

Through the day I thought
About what you did,
Why such anger over
something so small ?

But arriving home from work,
I entered the house to find
a small mosaic set on an old kitchen tile,
of a gold stemmed rose
unfolding under a pale blue sky.
Then I understood something
you must have known all along,

that only what is broken
has the chance to become
something wholly new in this world.

Sweet Tea Mysteries

Elmast Kozloyan

She slept in a bed filled with goat men
Limbs tangled into an anthropomorphic blob
Their soft tuffs of fur and faint bleating lulled her to sleep
only to be tossed out with one swift kick
She had grown accustomed to the bruises and shedding
Dryads living in the box plants
spun ivory webs around her bare skin
The sirens insisted they bathe her
she opted for a centaur rosewood oil massage
Outside the giants were harvesting
bleeding pomegranates
honeysuckle nectar
sacred lotus root
She walked past it all until she reached the car
Hermes had glued gold feathers onto her shoes
Her change of clothes were covered in opalescent dust
She cleaned them off and drove away

He waited for her in the coffee shop
Chatted over poppy seed bagels and sweet tea
He never questioned the glitter on her face
dark curls of hair in her sweater
or why she never took him home
He would never believe
no matter how much she wished he could

Late Shift & The swallows come

Thomas R. Thomas

Exhausted from working the late shift
at Union Bank in downtown LA,
Barbara Jean lies down on the couch.

Watching Tommy sitting on the floor -
lost in his own world playing with
the same toy for hours.

Opening her eyes - Tommy is gone.
Frantically, Barbara searches the
neighborhood, finding him watching the
Mickey Mouse Club with one of his girlfriends.

Forty years later and she still
feels the same guilt as she
looks into Tommy's eyes -
no longer lost.

***

the swallows come on
our birthday – in small bunches
at first — to scope it out

as if they would not be welcome
I sit alone — long for you

July 1970

Sarah Thursday

You seem taller in the trees
hair parted, hanging long as limbs
How high do you climb—
how long do you remain
among the leafless branches
Twenty year-old girl
newly mothered,
you must feel young smiling
Quilted dress doesn't stop you climbing
you stand up and lean over down
It is dusk on another day
you swing—arms open—in the forest
fingers spread wide
thick red cardigan
You must feel free
I only knew you this way
homemade dresses and open-toed shoes
you hate feeling closed in
You came back for your child
you must know
as the woods darken
a new decade is upon you
a chance to begin again
The mountain air, crisp
I imagine, fills your lungs slow
Head tilts back as you swing
back, smiling, and
swing forward

To Be Leppy

Manuel Gutierrez

I see Leppy's small bumpy head popping out
of the plastic tree in the terrarium on my shelf and I smile.
The monetary value of the lizard is $34.99
at the PetCo. The nutritional value is 200 calories, 35g protein.
It has the intrinsic value of an expensive chicken tender.

I can talk to Leppy but it will never
talk to me. It will never
read John Milton or William Shakespeare or Gertrude Stein.

If I slide open the mesh top of the cage and move
the plastic tree and put the lizard
in my hand it will not recognize
me. It will not see me as familiar,

it will not see me as family.
The lizard will never love me. I love the lizard. I would cry
if it were stepped on or bitten or starved.

There is an unquantifiable value in it
that cannot be shed biweekly like old dry skin.

Five other lizards have been named Leppy.
It has stopped being a name
and has become an archetype.
Leppy exists on a Platonic plane
and not in a terrarium. This Leopard Gecko
is not a specimen of the species
(Eublepharis macularius)
but a conduit for the concept
(Leppy.)

There is nothing to peer at me from above
and project a meaning onto me.
I am not the archetype
(Manuel.)

I am not a representation of Manuel
and there is no Existential catalog I can skim
through to pick out what I will project.

I am a human-lizard
with a strange thought.

Cranking

Olivia Somes

Beat a dead horse, beat her loud and proud
on Sunday morning in front of a pancake house,
because sometimes the only thing better
than syrup-slopped buttery hotcakes is a
diversion from the expected, the resurfacing cage
and haven't the yokels of history class figured out
it's more about the beating than the horse,
it's more about the hair-pulling, the sore throat
in the morning after sloshing on theory all night.
It's immunity. It's pain battling exposure to more pain.
Cranking the lever of vernacular warriorism is how
we learn to bold our words, to not scratch out our eyes
over the opening of a mouth, to realize our voice boxes
are not kumquats and can handle the pressure
of an audience with rifles and eardrums
waiting for their turns to say what must be said.

No Samaritan

Sean Gunning

I went down Wardlow to Woodruff yesterday
and saw a man lying on his side on the sidewalk,
his torso in a bird of paradise landscaped verge
between Ralphs parking lot and the sidewalk,
and the man and the landscape almost blended
into suburban invisibility.

"There was a man who went down
from Jerusalem to Jericho, and bandits
attacked him and robbed him and beat him
and left him with little life remaining in him,
and they went away."

At his side, I passed through the pungent death-cloud:
not a physical or spiritual death,
but a death of determination to keep striving.
Beaten down.
Born into desolation.
And I recognized the smell of the grace of God.

"And it chanced a priest was going down that road
and he saw him and passed on."

I prayed to our father, the father of us both,
I'm no better man than he, just more blessed.
Fortunate to be married, to have a home,
to have the worries and the unfulfilled dreams that I do.
I'm no better man than he, just more blessed.
And I knew it was not enough.
And I passed on...
not wanting to be late for an appointment.

"And likewise a Levite came and arrived at that place
and saw him and passed on."

And I prayed to our mother, the mother of us both.
And I reclined in the contoured dentist's chair
thinking it poetic that he resembled Doctor Roe,
with his black hair and black beard
and grey and black clothes,
and I resolved to look more closely
if he was still there on my way back.

"But a Samaritan as he journeyed came where he was
and when he saw him he had compassion on him.
And he came to him and bound up his wounds
and poured on them wine and oil,
and he brought him to the inn and took care of him.
And in the morning, he took out two pennies
and gave them to the innkeeper
and said to him, take care of him,
and whatever you spend more,
when I return I will give it to you."

And he *was* still there.
Now lying north-south, with his arms straight at his sides
and his feet crossed over thick grey socks
with a gaping hole at the ankle.
And his face was ashen-brown or olive-colored
or a shade of white or black.
And his beard was scraggly and tangled
and sorely lacking the dark, designer dashes of Doctor Roe's.
And he was lying on Woodruff Boulevard at 1:30 in the afternoon,
with closed eyes inside a grimy-grey hoodie-shroud
listening to the faint sound from the other side of the street
of the L.A. River carrying discarded debris back to sea,
and the faint footsteps of the people passing by.
And I passed by, and prayed for him a second time,
knowing it was not enough.
Knowing I was no Samaritan.

3 Haiku in March

Graham Smith

open mic at the north pole
santa smoked a bowl
and, eyes twinkling, read a poem from
his naughty list

the tragical presidency of william henry harrison
in this haiku play
the curtain rises, and the
prologue is the end

childhood memory
the old door-to-door
scissor sharpener man was
missing four fingers

Blood

LeAnne Hunt

"Children are vampires," my friend said.
After the park... the fair... the festival... the zoo... the circus...
the pool party... the play dates...and the birthday parties,
we sprawl in our chairs, like wilted prom corsages
three days after the deflowering and no phone call.
Our daughters whip around us like kites in hurricanes.

I cannot agree.

Children suck the marrow from bones, leach the color from hair,
bleach the skin and drain the life force at its source.
Vampires take only your blood, drink it down and stop;
children take your life and carry it forth.
All of your sins, half of your traits and three-fourths of your gestures
passed on like a virus replicating beyond control.
Vampires are kinder; they provide an end stop to your line.
Children run on and on.

Hell in Your Heart

Tamara Madison

In the therapist's office
the walls vibrate with sorrow
the carpet is briny with tears
the path from door to couch
is rutted by fear's footprint
and anger swirls like a ghost.
This is where you drop
your burdens when you open
your bag of secrets and let
the beasts out so the ugly ones
can howl and be free and stop
their crazy banging
at the hell in your heart.

Why Did We Domesticate a Thing Like Love?

Anna Badua

for MD + Artie + all other wild cats

There is a force that cannot be contained
If caged
would be a clawed arm
bleeding neck
a thrashing until let free
It is the spotted crooked tail
of the wild cat running the street
rummaging through garbage cans
the near miss of a moving tire
the loud hiss at a barking dog
It is not just the rubbing of legs
a flop and show of soft belly
not a jump in the arms
and a purr so loud
you feel a buzz in your chest
It is the slink of muscle
the sideways glance and flinch
as you reach for it
It is the jump off a two-story building
It is traversing the underlings of cars
Once cornered
black rimmed
copper eyes
large pupils
staring
hair on end
It is the backing away
and watching the wild cat
run the street
and simply
letting things
be

Monday's Child

Barbara Eknoian

He arrived five days before my first birthday
so I learned to share early. Mama said I was
Friday's child loving and giving.
As toddlers we slept in a double bed.
He drew an imaginary line and warned,
"Don't cross it."
At camp, I spent my allowance carefully
so on the bus ride home I'd have a treat.
The lady at the snack window said,
"Sorry your brother used up your money."
I was a spelling bee whiz,
he was dyslexic.
Every lunch hour, Mama played a record
and we'd hear, "A-Apple B-Banana,"
but phonics escaped him.
Most teachers called me into his class
to take home notes to my mother.
He dropped out of school,
related to the Hippie movement,
experimented with drugs, tried LSD,
and stayed with marijuana.
He was Monday's child, fair of face.
When he walked into a crowded room,
someone said, "He's beautiful.
With that beard he looks like Jesus."
He surpassed me reading Philosophy,
hated to hear about the imbalance
of power in the world.
Football players and Johnny Carson
making millions made him go into a tirade.
He could've out-talked the radio hosts.
Now he lives at a shelter, and called me to say
he contracted HIV from a lady he'd been with.
I'm horrified thinking she probably tricked him,
but he says,
 "No, we were just two lonely people
out drinking, who need a warm body to feel close."

I could not

Fernando Gallegos

I could not live by the Cliffs of Moher
The Atlantic would call to me to join it's crashing waves

I could not cross Pont Nuff
The Seine would whisper *Je t'aime pour toujours*

I could not stand near the Gullfoss waterfalls
The vertigo would set in, I would join the deep unknown

I could not walk amongst the thorn forest
My blood would feed the dirty earth

I could not live amongst the clouds
My wingless-body would of gravity feel

I could not lie beside you
Your siren calls would silence me

the igneous palms of California

Karie McNeley

lie listening for hours to the tongues of political dogs
lapping our fortunes cheap like crystal balls
in a silver spade locket around our necks
like a tight noose choking away our breaths
heavy and bold once, but now stuttering
and twitching like a bird near death
in the middle of an open road, a wingless plane
crash landing into an abyss of forest
green eyes blinded as we burst and shatter
into vexed confetti fragments, smoking
like a slow chimney towards the clouds
whisked and wispy and then chased away
from the sky by our powerful orange
mushroom boom, deafness followed by
press-board particles and grey cement
from our blood-soaked houses, dripping
wet and sloppy; beach sand to drip castle,
from the igneous palms of the California coast
to Atlantic waves clacking and chiming
like rhythm to the sub-Mediterranean wind
as we await our indefinite tsunami quake fate
listening for hours to the tongues of mangy dogs
lapping our fortunes cheap like crystal balls
in a patriotic locket around our necks,
red, white, and blue choking away our breaths.

Our Mother

Manuel Gutierrez

The Earth, wrapped in a towel, waits for her rape kit
in the police station. The rainforest is a yellowed sweater
laying in the alley; moth-bitten brown holes were once green
hand stitching done by your grandmother.

A Missouri congressman assures
us that the Earth has a way of shutting
things down if it was actually a Legitimate Rape™.

They jizzed oil all over the sea birds
and tried to use dawn soap to hide the evidence.
The polar bears have been shat on and are homeless
because the white knitted icecaps are being nervously unraveled.

God has damned us to this crime scene.
The didgeridooing whales sing our requiem
because we've killed the Earth and NASA's been defunded
so we're all stuck here damned
to incinerate with the naked corpse of the Earth.

Cons in Prose: A How-to Guide

JL Martindale

Step up to the podium.
Take a deep breath.
Close your eyes,
(maybe bow your head?)
Flip through your chapbook
or loose-leaf pages
marred with courier type-face
pulled from a new-retro-peechee.

Preface
Everything
with un-necessary
background.

Clear your throat,
        and

Begin.

Tell yourself:
the audience seeks guidance
in your oration
they crave epiphanies
in each carefully culled word,
each
_ pain-
        stakingly
_____ placed
_____ pause
and prudently planned
Em
    FAH
sis.

This collective
connects

in seemingly candid
consonance.

Leave them
with life altering
lessons
in alliteration.

Close with humor:
irony is poignant.

- Fini -

Let them clap.
Act humbled.
Maybe you should blush.
(but not too much.)

Now peddle those books.

Inspire(!)
your admirers.
Tell them:
they too can write poetry as well as you
...Some day.

Smile.
No one will notice:
like pop lyrics without music,
like glam-rock without pyrotechnics,
your mute words
lay lifeless
on that pilfered
(office) paper.

Defying Physics

Raundi Moore-Kondo

On the most unromantic of afternoons
you and I came together
like the gusts of wind off the Puget Sound
and the Tacoma Narrows Bridge.

We were complicit deadly chemistry,
set to self-destruct. Not by design—
but by our combined essence.

I'd been born into bondage
and was willing to lose limbs
for a few sweet reverberations of freedom.

You wore my rhythms like instinct
and committed seduction at a nuclear
and unconscionable level.

Tuning into me like hi-def,
crystal-clear radio. Filtering out
every frequency apart from mine.

Your decisive search for harmonics
made for the slightest damping.
It was exquisitely timed foreplay
meant only to prolong the violence.

Your tones exhumed new depths
in me and caused my crests to sky-rise.
When your vibrato plied at my wavelengths
they spread themselves apart and wide.

Willing, but completely unprepared
to be ravaged and consumed
by the synergy of our mutually-exclusive,
ever-heartening amplitude.

The resonance was fleeting.
It was our dissonance that caused me to break
so unevenly.

All that writhing and twisting
was just another way to escape
the structure that contained me.

Like Solomon's most misinterpreted song,
your timbre degraded and dissolved
during my demolition.

You were nothing more than a cunning linguist
armed with a lethal aero-elastic flutter.

I tried to defy physics and became life imitating
natural disaster—
an act of God.

I tore myself apart to become one with you,
to become something new.
If only there'd been a beautiful sound
to crumble into.

None will vanish. Many will appear.

AJ Urquidi

after two weeks the phallocentric
               nap of youth concluded
every herb garden sprouted
        an oil well

digging a foxhole in the crawlspace
               below the living room
the child found a missing jawbone
               of a movie starlet extra
      from *North by Northwest*
tale articulators swarmed the carnal
       suburb for two weeks

          until one night they stampeded
the alley to the topiary plot behind
          the tattoo clinic where a live
oak's thirty-second highest branch
       curled into the silhouette of La Virgen
          de Guadalupe

in the latitudinal township across
          the peninsula uninterested
oil dragons reared their iron skulls
       returned to their feeding
then looked slowly again at each
             falling palm frond

         until one night when the child
passed in blooming ruckus
         the motionless motors
      no longer sighed
           just crouched
dead beasts into themselves

Praying

Mickie Lynn

Hands clasped in prayer
kneeling at the alter
– begging –
the homeless make their nickels
to buy their smokes
but still wear filth
and find food in the garbage
like the landfill feeds the seagulls
and the beach provides shells to
crabs that outgrow their old homes
in the shallow tide pools
full of sea anemones and cucumbers
that the children poke at
in fascination
as the parents look on
quietly thanking God for their blessings.

Park Bench Behind the Diamond

Marcus Clayton

"Fall in love and get married then boom
How the hell did it get here so soon?" -Tom Waits

On the other side,
of the viridescent fence—
upturned chain-link at the feet
trench too small
for our torn
sneakers to sneak under—
are children
children, children.
Little capsules of verve
play soccer with their hands
goalie covers home plate
girls shove boys, boys
laugh at their grated knees
smiling without rules
without the disconcerted
knowledge that, "you
gotta use your feet."

Thankfully, we can't
crawl under the fence
to warn them, as we sit
cracked statues holding each
other's frost tipped hands,
only stare forward
finding rust over the green
holes within the links,
weak as bended bone,
our shoulders touch only
to bridge ants, my free
hand warmer in pocket
fingering loosed thread, ring
finger buried under lint.
We could leave if we didn't pretend
that we forgot how to use our feet.

The Poets' Party

Terry Wright

And there you are, hulking, for there is no other word for it, you are
hulking in your bulk: your bulk hulks: you are a black

raincloud in that room, a bulbous, billowing storm front of black clouds
and of course the promise of green electric lightening.

And then what a sea rush of oceanic feelings in me; you are still there.
You haven't changed! How far back this You goes!

We could still be friends. It could happen. We could make jokes about
thin-fingered poets with their facial hair and artfully

disheveled clothes. I see the cracks and the ways I could worm
into you until our friendship blurted out of a crack like a dirty city flower.

I could get in there; I see the crack. And at the same time
I recognize the frantic worm-turning I have to do in order to find a way

back to you, back to your side, to be sitting on that bed
next to you, hissing whispers into your little seasnail ear.

Investigating Acquaintances

Olivia Somes

A cheap bodega, three years ago,
Sunset or Silverlake, five PM or nine,
buddy of yours went by last name only,
Palmeri, some parroted generalizations
about hipsters and Jack Kerouac,
Gorgonzola and black merlot,
a box cutter turtled out your back pocket,
we'd throw around the word *friends*.
A year earlier, at Microcosms, a thrift
slash head shop, the owner's mustache
moved like a seesaw as he spit chew,
his name, Clark or Kent. You rifled
through incense like a maniac for thimbles.
You scored a Ziploc of screens. You were
queer then or just loose on pills, vegan
every Wednesday, we'd throw around
the word *friends*. A year before that
you were a chick at Pedonne's pizza,
picked off the olives, scraped the foam
from your Hefe with a butter knife, black
nail polish, a vernacular for the strange,
Tarot cards and toe rings. *Friends*.
Six months before that you're forty-something,
played keyboard in some big local band, *The Frames*,
twenty years ago, clothes like ashtrays,
MOM tatted on your forearm,
a habit for saying *you know what I mean*.
Friends. A month before that, you're pregnant
seventeen, glittered face, pink flip flops,
cheese dogs at the mall, cellphone never
leaves your hand. *Friends*. A week
before that, you're a lifeguard by day,
bomber by night, paint stained fingertips,
jeans cut to shorts, a meek mustache,
bum beers from guys in front of 7-11,

Fuck the Police. Friends. A day
before that it was yesterday, you're
a couple, at a hookah bar, both tall, matching
kicks, blue thick laces, peach tobacco,
love making plans for tomorrow,
hiking and cheap tacos. *Friends.*
An hour before that: a bed, windows, walls,
—pieces of a moment strummed together,
fantasies out of acorns.

The Taos Egg Incident

Clifton Snider

I have been one
hit by an egg in Taos, New Mexico,
walking a two-lane, lightless
residential street at night,--
my black windbreaker splattered
with fragments of shell stuck on,
yolk and whites, my glasses too,
camera case, leg & shoe.

I blame an SUV
or rather a restless kid
in this beautiful one-paseo town,
cruising with his buddy
equipped to cure their boredom
with an egg, organic I suppose
(this *is* Taos, after all). He threw
it at the first stranger passing by,
threw it hard as a baseball
just above my heart.
                    —*22 August 2005*

Quarter 4:
May, June, July

Lemon Cake

Sean Moor

I imagine that there will be an open mic at your funeral
2 poems or 5 minutes, whichever comes first
You, of course, will be the featured reader

Still, 15 minutes of silence, can feel like 15 months
that's an awful lot to ask of the *iPhone* generation
I don't know what you were thinking
Maybe you've become practiced at saying nothing
or, perhaps, that's just how you say goodbye.

You've moved on, but the rumors persist
that you haven't really left this world
Recently, there have been unconfirmed sightings,
apparitions that rattle the chains of my spectral heart

I, myself, saw someone who looked exactly like you
seated at a poetry reading
your arms wrapped tightly around your body
your right hand on your left shoulder
reaching back, but not for me

I could see the crook of your finger
where it was broken and never healed
I could smell the rotten tooth in your mouth
I could feel the burning scar of the child we lost

But I knew that you weren't the woman that I loved
because they spelled your name wrong
on your Starbucks cup

And maybe you were never the woman that I loved
because love can be a kind lie
the type that you tell your yourself
because you really want it to be true
because you really need it to true
because you've waited your whole life
for that one person who completes you

But it turns out that everything good is already inside you
and no one can complete you
because that's work that you must do for yourself

Drowning In Your Blue

Raundi Moore-Kondo

My pockets are so full of your blue
it is seeping through the seams of my jeans
and running down my legs.

I need a mop.

You have made a mockery of rain gutters
staining the rafters, and dissolving sheetrock,
before heading out to become lost in the sea.

I want to grind the grime embedded under your nails
between my teeth.
I crave the taste of your clawing
and the collateral damage
of your escape.
Your panic.
Your adrenaline and rebellion.
Your hard work, poor hygiene
and the sweat and skin of women
you'd swear you never loved
as much as you loved me.

I swallowed the last eyelash
you left on my pillow,
that little piece of you went down
so easy, tasteless, and whole.
I can still feel it.

Warm Sake Does Not Agree with You

LeAnne Hunt

In winter, I drink sake hot to heat my blood. All I see
clouds as from a sauna's steam. The puffs I exhale
are dragon smoke, and I mythical. I chew cinnamon
until my mouth burns, but still I shiver. Sake wraps
around me like a shawl.

Pour until it spills over the *masu* onto a saucer. It is
my Fountain of Youth and warms the spring at my basin. I
forget, when it sings siren melodies in my blood, these
years of dry want, the cold hearth, the bare cupboards
and the wasteland of my bed. I twine a lock of midnight
around my finger and remember fire.

ante meridiem VIII
savoring the butterscotch intervals
between seconds of non-sextions

ax NTP

my belly is an old dryer, your touch
is an even older pair of grey vans,
thump. thump. when you draw

lines of suspension on my hungry-is-
not-a-strong-enough-word-for-this-skin,
is it more or less suggestive to tessellating

frayed nerves? e-late. illicitations. your top lip
arch is a heron mid-wing-flap, shawling
tripwires of potential. to unpack our eager

fancy now would be clumsy,
pedestrian. i am a mullet, fawning
for symmetry, at best, waiting for the jump.

the inflections in your sighs cut
off at just the ripe angle of 83 degrees, they slant
unto me, into me, thicker than calligraphy,

more percolating than pulmonary veins.
i'm not the initial soot, but leftover
soot on side furnaces of brick buildings.

your body, three quarters of a winter's night,
your body, three quarters of a winter's night,
i could sleep in the cold of you

Jawbone Siphon Song

Frank Kearns

"There it is. Take it." William Mulholland

Bart drove Sarah up Three Ninety Five
then North away from the two lane blacktop
on the unmarked graded road

to where steel pipe as wide as an automobile
bends up eight hundred fifty feet
a giant "V" carved on canyon walls

They stood on the warm steel in the sun
and felt the heat work into their shoes
felt the vibrations under their feet

and heard the Jawbone Canyon Siphon's
hum   almost inaudible above
the desert sounds and silences.

Bart talked cubic feet per second
incompressible fluid and the pressure
of a column of water towering high

and Sarah listened but listened too
to the song from inside the arched metal tube
as the water raced passed hoop joints and rivets

echoes of flowers in Onion Valley
and trickles from glaciers nestled in
the granite slopes of the Palisades

she heard the scratchy resonance of dried out fields
and the patchwork patter of bought up farms
the talk of armed men at the aqueduct gates

and a mantra of names
Eaton Mulholland Lippincott
Otis San Fernando Los Angeles

a chant repeated by the wind
as it picked the salt and sand
from the dry bed of Owens lake

and twirled them across the empty flats
to sift through the hollow windows and doors
of the broken-down sheds of Olancha

Moon Mother

Raquel Reyes-Lopez

I spat on the moon to shine her. She told me thank you.
It was the closest thing to affection she ever had.
I curled in her crater afterward and vented out
my earth burdens.

I shared with her the story of how my human heart
broke, my pain weighed her down like a pregnancy,
but as a surrogate mother would she decided
to continue carrying me.

So I regrew my umbilical cord, attached it to her smile,
and nourished myself off her moonlight glow. Nine months
it was her, the stars, and me. She questioned what would she do
when it was my time to go?

While I regenerated the broken parts of me with her love,
she glanced at Earth with envy, cursing at it quietly, but only
when I wasn't kicking her with my agony. It was so unfair
she thought.

I would die on Earth and she would never have me again.
Despite the care she has given. She wouldn't be able to see me
fall in love, for good this time, with a man who adored the Moon
first, before he learned to love the Sun.

Attachment, what she couldn't afford, just happened. It was the night
when she glanced at my fragile flesh, noticed the vulnerability
I carried for being human, and she engorged red with empathy.
I had become her moon child.

On my last month with her she couldn't take it anymore.
She shook soft sadness and developed phases of withdrawal:
becoming Dark Moon, Waxing Crescent, Half Moon
incomplete pieces of herself.

I woke up. It was my last day with her. She cut my umbilical
cord herself. Her energy had healed me completely. I jumped
off her gravitational pull, told her thank you, and said my good bye
as I floated back to Earth.

Now before bed I speak to her through frequencies. She listens,
plays my transmissions over and over, becoming the envy
of the galaxy as space hears my broadcasting
dedicated only for her:

Thank you for everything. I will always be your moon child.
As you will always be my moon mother. Would you kindly
heal my children if they ever visit you? The same way
you healed me in ways Earth never could.

I Took James Joyce To A Bar In Long Beach

Charlotte San Juan

We were booth-stuffed beneath the
clatter-clamor of harsh bar chiaroscuro,
He was coughing fits of *Chamber Music*
open handed phlegm-hack, readjusting
his eye-patch, raised his glass with a toast
to "bid adieu to girlish days."
And over in the corner by the arcade games,
in the wheezing and bickering sound bytes
and blinking lights
a woman's inked neck and shoulders
rolled slow with the song in her head
her spritzed curls damp in the sweat-light
she was the leaning, love-struck drunk
of her own late thirties, pining over
chance, over the smoke-flirt-kiss
of lost men. She was the tip-toed
damaged damsel guarding the jukebox,
the heroine of the night,
amidst the dizzy sway of plastic-paper
shamrocks and too-ra-loo-ras
over the sports commentating flat screen
heads talking, necks bar stool swiveling
back and forth, caught in the ivory-corn
grin of old men and their spreading
crows feet, beneath the stolen banter
speaking in waves of Long Beach
poured poetry, of her tight jeans
cupping her with sequins,
of the clink of glasses giving away
the condensation of secrets, all
talk and thick skin and hard lips
and tales from the laundromat
hanging from the shadows of her
eyelids, an anklet around her
inked rosary, spelling Frailty

thy name is woman in the
links of an unpolished silver
chain pilfered from a pawn shop
love affair, she was the swooning
aftermath of Wednesday nights
beneath the neon, still hair-twirling
in hopes for something more than
insignificant, insomniac embraces from
somebody's stepped-out-for-cigarettes
husband, who will take her to pace
*under the moongrey nettles, the black
mould and muttering rain*, only to leave
her in the same weeded vacant lot
of last week, before her eyes could
ever *gather simples of the moon.*

For Aldehyde

Raquel Reyes-Lopez

There's a half sheet of blank paper crumbled
in your father's pocket. I got a pen in my purse
somewhere. That's if I haven't lost it.

April came. Two lines revealed you were mine.
Your father would twirl me in the kitchen.
As the eggs fried we discussed
whether you would be a girl
or a boy. I felt complete.

I was whole with you inside of me.
One afternoon at the prick of a needle
a fractured dream landed heavy on sand.

> hCG 70,000
> hCG 13,352
> a week passed
> hCG 9,000
> and another
> hCG...0

My body is a hormonal tidal wave in flux.
Aldehyde, I'm trying to breach the barriers
of a shore where we're not allowed to touch
to say good-bye.

I know I am not alone in this.
I look at the moon teary eyed.
In the freckles of the Cosmos
there is a communal hymn
ringing for those of us
who have miscarried.

We Were the Tide
or Mom steps onto Long Beach Boulevard

J.D. Isip

Headlights swerved past you
big and white
small and red
glowing and floating
graceful steel bodies
upstream
downstream
your favorite black negligee
Seagram's 7, your favorite escape
bare feet on asphalt
bare legs in traffic

Twin boys in Underoos, six and skinny
eyes wide open
mouths wide open
waving in the frames between cars
Goodbye
Come back

I have felt the same draw
that solves the jigsaw self
by gathering the pieces
and tossing them away

Come back
Goodbye
We alternate in the aftermath
victim mother
villain mother
Two men in their thirties, stuck on the scene

menaced by your mania
fortified by your fears
constructing our favorite versions

variations on the scope of your destruction
numb to pain
numb to love
graceful steel bodies
glowing and floating
small boy hearts
big boy lives
desperate to swerve past you

Your eyes were looking for him,
your outstretched hands wanting
a man, a life that the tide
ever pulled you from

Goodbye, you said
Come back, we said

neurosity XXXVIII
emergency exit

Jax NTP

embrace
what may
or may not
be the reception
of cowardice

rat droppings
and expired
orange juice

what happens
to *waldo*
when you
find him?

the safe
word is
boysenberry,
not olallie

alarm will sound
faster, faster

then without
hesitation
linger

what keeps
on — divides

the crickets
are salty
on her lips

the key,
what is
broken

Friday's Inflections

I let you borrow
                              my voice
            and this is how
                        you treat it?
                  Lost—misplaced—
a revenge opera closed-

            captioned, silent
                              but deadly.
            Thought I heard
                        it on a billboard,
                  now too faint
a sound to recall.

            Our needles
                              no longer
            in the groove,
                        the new noise
                  is more entertaining.
Anything I say can

            and will be used
                              in your mouth.
            Our callouses make me
                        laugh because no one
                  taught me how
to behave. I'll work

            it out, jog at dawn in
                              my blasphemy
            jacket. I see it
                        hovers yet at thirty
                  thousand feet.
I'll have to remind myself

to find my words

                                        by Wednesday.

                Thought I heard

                         them in the microwave—

               now too they are molds

of jell-o draped in ventriloquist's cloaks.

At the Country House One Sunday in Provence

Tobi Cogswell

Pears and honey—
des poires et de miel—
sweetness that transcends
a language meant to know in the bones
as I know in my bones.

When is a glance not a glance,
but a living history, a hand to the cheek,
viens ici, the crust of a bread
cracking the family tree? Salt.
No salt. I can afford to keep you,
or I can't.

Let's have some sugar.
Let me taste from your lips
the things we do not say.

I wear a green dress.
You see my legs through the silk.
They are not frightened, they are
one, two, strong, and standing
in front of you—a dare, not
an acquiescence.

Write me a letter *en français, peut-être
en anglais,* it does not matter. I want
to feel each stroke of your pen
as if a caress.

Des poires et de miel under glass.
An antique table and Mozart in the courtyard—
a window so high, we don't know
if it's someone playing,
or an old-fashioned phonograph.

Gentle the pins from my hair,
your hand finds the back of my neck.
A sweet kiss, another crust of bread.
Let's stir our coffee and grow old.

Serving Fresh Fish

Peggy Dobreer

I am from spinning in circles and rolling down hills
from kickball in the cul-de-sac till streetlights come on
I am from ally ally oxen...
I am from always free falling down tree climbing when curd
cuts through plaster flies up brackish stairwells
I am from damp basement smell of earth
door unbolted above my head
I am from avocado fruit supped off thick black skin
held in the bough of the mother tree
descended from one little alligator pear

I am from below sea level and jut above the eye
King Neptune was my invisible friend
His staff in hand we'd ride the tram from P.O.P.
get caught up with beatnik lesbians in tattoo galleries on the strand
Grandmother didn't like it not one bit
And it is not because of the way they dress
 I am from Bubby's rules
from Lifeguard Juniors keeping things safe
recycle aluminum bury washed up jelly fish
I am from picking up for others

I am from waves rolling in and slipping out
from glooming in the mist
I am from sun cuts through clouds takes off layers
oils tinted with iodine
I am from transistor radios on sand
sails trilling beyond break rocks
waves meeting at the top of the berm
a havoc of ocean foams between my toes
splashes up my thighs
I am from two fish flapping out of school
I am fresh from loving you

Shadow of the Swing Set

Robin Dawn Hudechek

I used to think if I swung high enough, fast enough
swing set chains would break free and lift me.
I could see the flat, hard playground drop below me in a molten square,
the laughter of children on seesaws, far below.

Up here, with seagulls, and wind that bends and rolls, I look down
at boys hanging from the rocket ship,
like primordial hunters missing only their spears,
with their poking and prodding, barring the door
with their bodies and fists. "EEEW retard!"
and "C'mon, here's the door, retard!"

Then I'm running again, always running across that same field
with its rusted fence with the spokes torn back,
separating my street from the school.
I always know, even with the pack of them,
nipping at me with their rabid catcalls,
if I could just reach that fence with its gaping hole,
they would stop, arms gangling uselessly,
then turn back,
as if that fence had some secret force field
or ray of death only I was immune to.

But more often, I stumble and fall
and they are upon me with their shoves and punches
or throwing stones, or sticks or balls
that land, as always, yards away.
This is my penance, I knew, even then,
for throwing rocks over my fence
into the next-door neighbor's pool.

An ancient softball lands at my feet, splitting at its skin and seams,
and later, when I turn it in my hands,
I wonder at the assailant who hurled it,
adjusting his aim to just miss me.
What did it cost him, this pretend hatred, his secret shame?

But even now, I am that child, that moth, pale and unlovely,
squirming within a prison of fear.
When the blows land, always in my stomach,
snuffing out breath and air--
I tell myself they will not hurt me, not really--
these bruises that bloom under my shirt,
tender to the touch, and sifting colors like puddles
under the press of my fingers before they fade,
never leaving marks anyone could see.

I would like to soar above their heads
but I cannot fly high enough or fast enough
to escape the playground where faces crowd around me,
and the bars of the rocket ship press into my back and thighs.

I could crouch,
evade the clawing hands,
and let the cement scrape my palms as I back out the iron door.
Or I could face them,
fists swinging in a satisfying rhythm,
catching first this boy, then that one, watching them fall back,
bars releasing their arms and legs like so many dismembered dolls.

But I do none of those things:
I am rooted firmly on the ground
alone in that field of yellowed grasses
with the rocket ship rusted and condemned:
playgrounds are much safer now—
so they tell me
and the shadow of a seagull's wing
passes high above me.

Remarking Upon Recent Photos of Myself

Alan Passman

Pear-shaped and ashamed at the muffin top atop
my upper torso, I remember and envision sitting
in an office while a nurse told me that the way
I got fat was a blessing in disguise. "It means
you can lose weight faster. If you were shaped
like an orange or something else round, then
you'd have a hard time taking it off." Nothing's
easy about what I carry around.

I'm married

to this fat because it is my proverbial ball and chain
and what I'd give to be shaped not like any sort of fruit,
but a man rather with bulging pecs and washboard abs
or a scrawny, spring chicken-like trunk. The proudly strutting
topless kind, the "Hey, it's hot even with the A/C on so let's

take our shirts off"-sort, or the "My nipples aren't overly
sexualized in this country, so I don't have to wear a shirt
if I don't want to"-physique. Not the "let's wear a t-shirt
to the swimming pool or the beach"-one. Not the "I'm too
broke to afford bigger clothes, so let's just look like we're
gonna burst out of the old ones"-variety. Not the "self-conscious
to the point of panic attack"-style either.

I want

to be sexy, to be adored, to be gawked at, to be fantasized about,
to be all things and everything, to be someone else. Not an edible
piece of vegetation, but a person.

Baddo-Daddo

Ris Fleming-Allen
for my mother

Dearest Mama,

You married a man
who pops the clutch and
corners via handbrake
    on his way to work.

What possessed you to think
he would ever give you
quiet
      and/or
           well-behaved offspring?

      No apologies, but
      all our love,
           Your Children

Sanction

Tobi Cogswell

Because I stand at the kitchen window slicing tomatoes.
Because my fingertips are numb as always.
Because you fasten my necklace because I can't.
Because your hands are broad and brown and gentle

Because birds are in the nest outside the front door.
Because you drink the olive oil from the tomato bowl.
Because we have no fountain, but we believe we have one.
Because the kitchen is painted Honeymoon Yellow.

Because I lift my hair on the back of my neck.
Because you say you will kiss me in any and all lights.
Because the evening clouds are sashed bronze from the fires.
Because you are a man of your word.

Note to My Younger Self on the Beauty of Birds

Larry Duncan

One day you will meet a woman
who will put her hands on your face
as if cradling a tea cup
to scry the leaves.
Her fingers will fit the damage
and petty brutalities
you wear like a roadmap
over the contours of your skin.
It will slow the ceaseless
rattle of your bones
and you will know a quiet
like you have never known.

When you think of her,
you will think of the color blue
coming in waves
not like water
but as if it were alive,
aware and all around you.

Do not reach for her wrist.

You will be too heavy
and there will be something
fragile in the air,
something you cannot help but crush
if you close your hand.

You will never wake together in the morning.
You will never read articles
from the Sunday paper to her
over bagels and coffee.
You will never come up on her at the kitchen
sink just as she brushes a strand of loose hair
behind her ear with a wet glove,
leaving suds on her cheek
like tiny clouds.

You will never know if your hand
fits her face as hers fits yours.

And she will never know
that you are slow moving and earthbound
that you are a stone
that you fall with weight
into a pit of gravity and hunger
that crushes the bird-boned brilliances
of your life into a constellation
of dense, misshapen diamonds.

Just be still
and she will fly away.

But one night,
if you're lucky,
she will lie in bed
and think of you
at the exact moment
you are seeing blue
and it will be as if you're standing
face to face
in a world without weight
and it might just be enough
to lift you up and off the ground.

and what's abundance to the ocean, anyhow?

Dan Steinbacher

In creation myths,
the earth is grown from a glop of ground
brought up from underwater.
Sometimes it's a turtle or toad that emerges,
a seed hatching from his dirt-stained head,
sometimes the gods do it,
presumably out of bored curiosity.

I like it best when it is a bird who dives deep,
flapping wings used as fins,
eyes darting,
wildly out of its element.
And when the raven,
(it must have been—
could only have been the raven)
bursts forth from the water
with a triumphant caw,
and the bit of runny, mossy mud in its beak
fell and immediately began to expand in the sudden
liquid gold light of the sun,
was the Ocean jealous?

Did it resent this newcomer's intrusion?
Or did it recognize the land as simply another part of itself
brought forth to the light,
remember the depths from which change must come,
and then embrace the baby Pangaea
on every side,
kissing her sandy forehead with each curling wave—
and in doing so did not the Sea
also cause itself to rise?

All the Young Men

Clifton Snider

They come in Pre-Raphaelite curls,
androgynous shoulder-length straight hair,
brown and blond, red and black;
they part their hair like boys,
like surfers, like curly-headed angels;
they razor-cut their sides, then plaster what's left
in rows on top, they make corn-rows,
crew-cut faces of youth, ears, napes,
divine military cuts, tails, spikes,
sideburns that command my eyeballs
like their earrings, their tank tops, tits,
shoulders, arms, their delicate masculine hands;
their denim, their leather, their slim, tight
trousers, their hairy legs, their toes,
their sacred feet; they walk like warriors,
like tender initiates,–they have no inkling
they are holy. Sacred as ancient herms,
they mark boundaries, invite devotees.

mayan nocturne
1:00 AM, 12/22/12

Kevin Kreiger

he thinks, watching the buddha
silhouette the balcony
soft & unperturbed — he thinks
that he is almost disappointed.

solstice halfmoon, night
still spinning in the face of heaven.

the nothing that never was.

foolish, yes, but he wondered
what it would be like
to disembody, to be
weightless at long last.

he will wake again later,
morning in its habitual
repose along the wall,
stretch sleepworn muscles
against the same faded sheets

as downstairs the cats,
who never once considered
the world was about to end,
gather around their bowls.

What You Need To Know About INFPs, Should You Ever Love One

Nancy Lynée Woo

They carry peace bombs in their foreheads. Ready to explode should you just extend one hand, nay, one pinkie finger to help lighten the load. The bomb builds back up again every night. Their dreams are of colors we can't yet see, and they are quiet builders, master blenders, mantis shrimp. When the whirring starts in the morning, you know someone is throwing all the colored fruits into the mix. Serving it to you like a rainbow juice from the other world, extravagant. Though, when the world is not those beautiful clouds from that beautiful dream, it's the deepest mud-brown from where she face plants into the waste stream. Some say wrap those red claws in rubber bands and throw it all into the boil. That's when the screaming starts. She starts to smell herself. All irrationalities become clearer than wood. Ready to stew. She is rotten, no good. Until. Your pinkie. Extends. And then, boom.

Cadence Collective:
Class of 2014
Yearbook Portraits

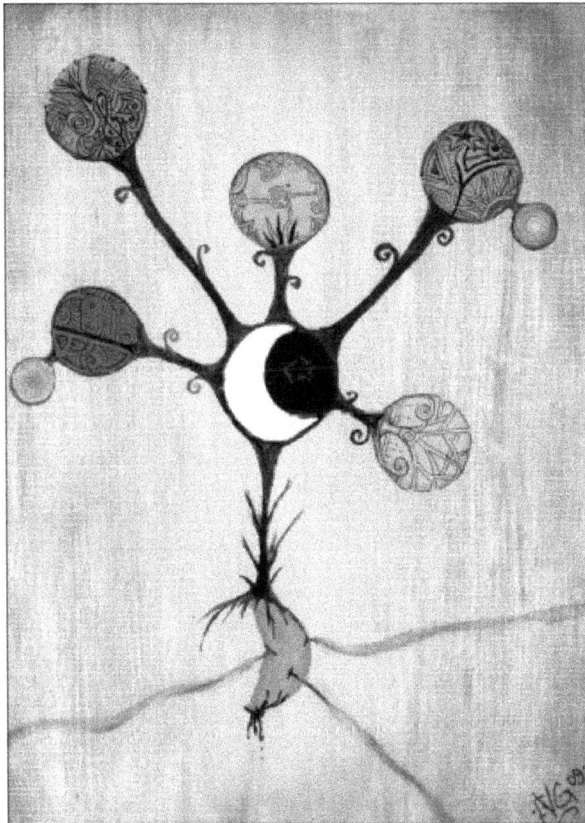

AJ Urquidi

Alan Passman

Alisha Attella

Anna Badua

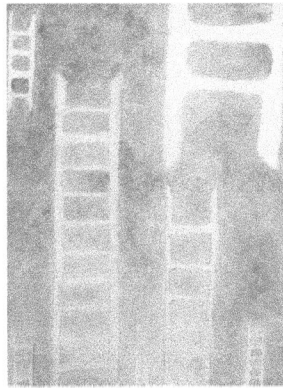

Athena

Barbara Eknoian

Charlotte San Juan

Christian Lozada

Clifton Snider   Clint Margrave   Dan Steinbacher

Daniel McGinn   Danielle Mitchell   Denise R. Weuve

Donna Hilbert   Elder Zamora

Elmast Kozloyan

Faith Gobeli

Esmeralda Villalobos

Fernando Gallegos

Frank Kearns

G. Murray Thomas

Graham Smith

J. D. Isip

Jackie Joice

Jax NTP

Jessica Claire Bennish

JL Martindale

John Brantingham

Karie McNeley

Kevin Clothier

Kevin Ridgeway

Kevin Kreiger

Larry Duncan

LeAnne Hunt

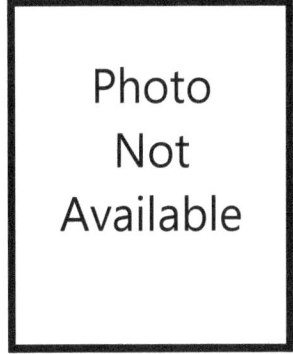

Manuel Gutierrez

Marcus Clayton

Marianne Stewart

Mickie Lynn

Nancy Lynée Woo

Olivia Somes

Peggy Dobreer

Raquel Reyes-Lopez

Raundi Moore-Kondo

Ricki Mandeville

Ris Fleming-Allen

Robin Dawn Hudechek

Sarah Thursday

Sean Gunning

Sean Moor

Sergei A. Smirnoff

Shannon Phillips

Steven Hendrix

Tamara Madison

Terry Wright

Thomas R. Thomas

Tobi Cogswell

Zack Nelson-Lopiccolo

Acknowledgments

The following have previously been published as listed:

AJ Urquidi "Friday's Inflections" in *Remedial Art Class*

Barbara Eknoian "Monday's Child" in *Westview: A Journal of Western Oklahoma*

Charlotte San Juan "I Took James Joyce To A Bar In Long Beach" in *Whittier College's Literary Review*

Clifton Snider "The Taos Egg Incident" and "All the Young Men" in *Moonman: New and Selected Poems* (World Parade Books)

Clint Margrave "A Poem Is Not A Teddy Bear", "My Father's Brain", and "Clenched Fists" in *The Early Death of Men* (NYQ Books)

Daniel McGinn "Everything Overlaps" in *1000 Black Umbrellas* (Write Bloody Press)

Denise R. Weuve "Laundromat" in *South Coast Poetry Journal* and "whore" in *Genre Literary Journal*

Donna Hilbert "My Heaven" in *Traveler in Paradise: New and Selected Poems*, "Old Man at the Pool" in *Deep Red*, and "Credo" in *The Green Salon*

Elder Zamora "If I Owned a Suit" in *Soundings Review*

G. Murray Thomas "Your Kidney Has Just Arrived at LAX" in *My Kidney Has Just Arrived*, "The Morning After" and "Love Vs. In Love" in *Cows on the Freeway*

Jackie Joice "King River Blues (Part One)" in *Song of San Joaquin* and *Green Grapes Black Hands*

Jax NTP "neurosity XII" in *Subliminal Interiors*, "ante meridiem VIII" in *The Fat City Review* and *Summer Anthology* (Silver Birch Press) and "neurosity XXXVIII" in *3:AM Magazine* and *The Art of Survival* (Kings Estate Press)

John Brantingham "Poem to the Child Who Was Almost My Son" in *Serving House Journal* and *The Green of Sunset*, and "Westminster Abbey, March 1991" in *The Green of Sunset*

Kevin Ridgeway "17th Street" in *Bank-Heavy Press: Robo-Book*, and "Tape Deck Blues" in *Turbulence (UK)*

Larry Duncan "Hank Williams Drives His Truck into a Tree" in *Black Heart Magazine*, "Bone-Yard Romance" in *Muddy River Poetry Review #7*, "Note to My Younger Self on the Beauty of Birds" in *Citizens for Decent Literature*, all in *Crossroads of Stars and White Lightning*

Marcus Clayton "Park Bench Behind the Diamond" in *Shark Reef*

Nancy Lynée Woo "Catwalk" in *The Camel Saloon*

Raundi Moore-Kondo "Defying Physics" and "Drowning In Your Blue" in
Let the Ends Spill Over Your Lips

Ricki Mandeville "Driving By the House I Grew Up In" in *King Author,*
"Ceremony" in *She Writes Anthology,* and "Winter Moon Pantoum"
in *A Thin Stand of Lights*

Sarah Thursday "July 1970" in *Healing the Heart of Ophelia*

Sean Gunning "No Samaritan" in *Verdad*

Shannon Phillips "Plum" in *My Favorite Mistake* (Arroyo Seco Press) and
"Eating" in *The Literary Review*

Tamara Madison "The Rose that Lupe" in *Crack the Spine*

Thomas R. Thomas "Late Shift" and "The swallows come" in *Five Lines,*
World Parade Books

Tobi Cogswell "The Ripening" in *Bellowing Ark,* "At the Country House One
Sunday in Provence" in *Spoon River Poetry Review,* and "Sanction"
in *Main Channel Voices*

Zack Nelson-Lopiccolo "Resurrección" in *Red Fez Magazine*

www.ingramcontent.com/pod-product-compliance
Lightning Source LLC
Chambersburg PA
CBHW052341100426
42736CB00047B/3403